THE PRENTICE HALL
Grammar Workbook

THE PRENTICE HALL
Grammar Workbook

Second Edition

Jeanette Adkins

Tarrant County Community College, Northeast

PEARSON

Prentice
Hall

Upper Saddle River, NJ 07458

Editorial Director: *Leah Jewell*
Executive Editor: *Craig Campanella*
Assistant Editor: *Jennifer Conklin*
Editorial Assistant: *Joan Polk*
Production Editor: *Julio Espin*
Prepress and Manufacturing Buyer: *Christina Helder*
Cover Art Director: *Jayne Conte*
Cover Designer: *Bruce Kenselaar*

Printed in the United States of America

10 9 8 7 6 5 4 3

ISBN 0-13-194771-0

Pearson Education LTD., London
Pearson Education Australia PTY, Limited
Pearson Education Singapore, Pte. Ltd
Pearson Education North Asia Ltd
Pearson Education Canada, Ltd
Pearson Educación de Mexico, S.A. de C.V.
Pearson Education—Japan
Pearson Education Malaysia, Pte. Ltd
Pearson Education, Upper Saddle River, New Jersey

❧ Contents ❧

Preface   vii
Pre-Test   1

1 Nouns   5
2 Pronouns   17
3 Regular and Irregular Verbs   37
4 Subject-Verb Agreement   52
5 Passive Voice and Consistent Verb Tense   60
   Review Test Chapters 1–5   68
6 Verbals: Gerunds, Participles, and Infinitives   70
7 Adjectives and Adverbs   79
8 Prepositions   102
9 Conjunctions   109
10 Exclamation   128
   Review Test Chapters 6–10   131
11 Fragments   133
12 Run-Ons   147
13 Dangling and Misplaced Modifiers   155
14 Parallelism   166
15 Punctuation   171
   Review Test Chapters 11–15   189
16 Numbers   193
17 Capitalization   208
18 Abbreviation   219
19 Troublesome Words   225

20 *Spelling*   237

Review Test Chapters 16–20   246

Appendix   248

Post-Test   256

Answer Key   258

❧ Preface ❧

The Prentice Hall Grammar Workbook is a diagnostic, prescriptive approach to mastering grammar, the mechanics of language, misused words, and spelling. This comprehensive workbook enables students to recognize and avoid potential errors as well as to resolve error problems. However, writing well involves more than recognizing and avoiding errors. It involves, to a great extent, understanding and internalizing how sentences work. To begin with, definitions in this workbook are followed by clear-cut examples. In addition, many practical applications are provided to lead students toward mastery of basic English sentence structure. By working through ample short practices, students begin to internalize the various sentence patterns and to write clear, mature, well-developed sentences. In Chapters 1 through 10, students are led systematically through the various parts of speech, including verbals. Students' writing skills are greatly enhanced when verbals are utilized. Chapter 11, "Fragments," and Chapter 12, "Run-ons," contain extensive practice because these are areas where students tend to have problems. Students must be able to recognize and write complete sentences before advancing to higher levels of writing.

In an effort to develop the ability to write mature and flexible sentences that reflect turns of thinking, students sometimes write misplaced and dangling modifiers. Chapter 13 contains exercises to help students learn to avoid or correct such modifiers as they may have slipped in during the composition. Chapter 14, "Parallelism," provides students with practice in presenting ideas in parallel patterns so that sentences flow smoothly. Therefore, students learn to put similar ideas in similar forms. Chapter 15, "Punctuation," is one of the most important chapters in this workbook. Sentences can convey a multiplicity of meanings, depending on how they are punctuated. Students become better writers when they have mastered the art of punctuating. Chapters 16, 17, and 18 provide extensive practice in the use of numbers, capitalization, and abbreviations. Chapter 19, "Troublesome Words," is specifically designed to point out and eliminate the improper use of commonly misused words. Chapter 20 covers the basic rules of spelling as well as a list of commonly misspelled words.

Included in this edition is a new appendix, English as a Second Language (ESL), which provides tips for non-native speakers. A pre-test, to be taken at the start of the course, and post-test, to be taken at the end of the course, as well as section tests for each group of five chapters have been added. The Answer Key has been updated to provide solutions for each of these new tests.

The Prentice Hall Grammar Workbook may be used in conjunction with a writing book, or it may be utilized solely as a comprehensive reference or grammar workbook.

Students need, and must develop, a strong command of English skills. This workbook, supported by guided practice and frequent application, will give students the tools to become better writers and speakers of English.

Jeanette Adkins

Pre-Test

A. Circle the appropriate answer for each sentence.

1. For (who, whom) do you plan to vote?

2. (You're, your) certain to fail if you keep making those snide remarks.

3. The children have not decided whether to go snorkeling, skating, or (to swim, swimming).

4. (Were, We're, Where) is the nearest convenience store?

5. All details must be fine tuned (real, really) soon.

6. To move (swift, swiftly) would prove beneficial.

7. The beeswax candles (cost, costs) a small fraction of her allowance.

8. She was oblivious (in, to) anything around her.

9. Not long ago, (you and I, you and me) shared the same dreams and aspirations.

10. A (1/8, one-eighth) inch screw fell through the crack, and we were unable to recover it.

11. Let's make a concerted effort (between, among) the three of us.

12. (Dr. morrison hughes, Dr. Morrison Hughes) impressed the vast audience with his dynamic dramatic interpretation of Porgy.

13. You (should of, should have) given him your undivided attention years ago.

14. (They're, their, there) anticipating something that will never transpire.

15. Janice is unconcerned, (but, nor) smart.

16. Both sets of dishes in that cabinet (is, are) dated before World War I.

17. It is (quiet, quite) impressive to see so many young people at the investment seminar.

18. (40%, Forty percent) of the instructors refused to participate in the extracurricular activities.

19. What is your (principle, principal) reason for such a challenge?

20. Have you seen any pictures dated in the (1800's, 1800s)?

21. Is March (13, thirteenth) an unrealistic deadline to propose?

22. My sister had over (19, nineteen) tumors inside her stomach.

23. One of the judges told Nguyen that his presentation was neither impressive (or, nor) informative.

24. I wonder (who, whom) left this beautiful leather belt in the restroom.

25. For the next 50 miles, this is a (two lane highway, two-lane highway).

26. All of the condominiums are vacant (accept, except) the one on the far end.

27. Why didn't you divide the crayons (between, among) the three of them.

28. Gloria has (fewer, less) marbles than Stanley.

29. Le Long wasn't feeling (good, well) yesterday.

30. I have (already, all ready) taken my medication for today.

B. *Insert commas and semicolons where needed. Mark the one sentence that is correct with a C.*

1. Order the pens, pencils, paper, staples, etc. from the bookstore.

2. The name of the newly formed company is Yancy Bates & Matson.

3. The results of the tests were inconclusive therefore the physician insisted on more testing.

4. The CEO was fired amid allegations of fraud the vice president kept his position.

5. The journal article, which received national acclaim, was discussed at length during the forum.

C. *Insert colons, quotations marks, hyphens, dashes, and apostrophes where needed.*

1. My answer on second thought is no.

2. *The American Novel An Historical Perspective* is available online.

3. Providing a biased opinion is like providing no opinion at all, said Jeremiah.

4. Mary demanded that her siblings do the following make beds, wash dishes, and vacuum the floors.

5. The womens basketball team is sensational.

6. Malcolm is the ex president of Foundations Abroad.

7. Some people spell Brittney, B r i t n e y.

8. The boys jacket was returned to the lost and found department.

9. My sisters in law articulated well at the annual oral competition.

10. That 18 wheeler almost sideswiped us!

D. Insert parentheses, underscores, diagonals, periods, question marks, and exclamation points where needed.

1. In case of an emergency, please equip your car with the following items: 1 a flash-light, 2 snacks, 3 a cell phone, and 4, a blanket.

2. Mail the package co Jonathan Lewis.

3. Give accolades to the editor of New Perspectives magazine.

4. Should you reciprocate because she bought your lunch yesterday

5. The FUBU Collection is still quite popular among teenagers

6. Gosh This road is dangerous.

E. Underline the verbals and verbal phrases in the following sentences.

1. Whistling and skipping are signs of happiness.

2. Pointing one's finger can have many different connotations.

3. To feign illness would be disadvantageous at this time.

4. Both of them, having recently moved into the neighborhood, feel like outsiders.

5. Reminiscing the good times can result in improvement of one's health.

F. Mark F for sentence fragments. Mark C for correct sentences.

_____ 1. Murky water standing in the birdbath.

_____ 2. Joycelyn sat quietly on the veranda and sipped her latte.

_____ 3. Thick fog surrounded the swamp adjacent to the gloomy mansion.

_____ **4.** Especially the ones with almonds in the center.

_____ **5.** Scouting in unknown territory in the middle of nowhere.

G. Mark F for fused sentences and CS for comma splices. Mark C for correct sentences.

_____ **1.** Consuella videotaped the panoramic view of Paris from the top of the Eiffel Tower, it was something to behold.

_____ **2.** The aroma of chestnuts roasting on an open fire permeated throughout the amusement park.

_____ **3.** Hawaiian Islands natives called Pearl Harbor the "Water of Pearl" a vast number of pearl oysters filled the harbor.

_____ **4.** On windy days, the gardens of the Castle of Versailles close winds escaping from the opening and closing of doors can damage precious paintings and sculptures.

_____ **5.** Bronze statues flanked the four corners of the enormous walls of the fortress, copper urns filled with richly colored flowers adorned the passageway.

❧ *1* ❧

Nouns

As you speak or write, you express your thoughts in words. Sometimes you may use only one word, such as *hello*. Usually, however, you use groups of words that make statements, ask questions, or give commands. Every word you speak or write has a definite use in expressing a thought or an idea. The way the word is used determines what part of speech that word is. There are eight parts of speech.

As you study and work through the exercises in this workbook, learn to recognize the parts of speech—the eight ways that words work for you as you communicate your thoughts and ideas to others.

nouns	verbs	adverbs	conjunctions
pronouns	adjectives	prepositions	interjections

UNDERSTANDING NOUNS

Nouns name things. They name the objects you see around you—perhaps a desk, a chair, or a tree. Your own name is a noun. Nouns also name things that you cannot see, such as your thoughts or ideas. You can learn to recognize nouns in three ways: by learning the definition of a noun, by studying the classes of nouns, and by learning the features that distinguish a noun from other parts of speech. In this chapter, you will study and practice each of these ways to identify nouns.

DEFINING NOUNS

A *noun* is the name of a person, place, thing, or idea.

CLASSIFYING NOUNS

- There are two classes of nouns: *proper nouns* and *common nouns*. *Proper nouns* name specific, unique persons, places, or things. They begin with a capital letter. All other nouns are called *common nouns*. They do not require a capital first letter.

- Nouns may be either *concrete* or *abstract*. A *concrete noun* names something that can be perceived through the senses (an object such as a *ship* or the *Queen Elizabeth II*). An *abstract noun* names a quality, a thought, or an idea (such as *courage* or *talent*).

    Persons (concrete nouns):   firefighter, people, Diana, American

    Places (concrete nouns):   school, park, Pentagon, museum

    Things (concrete nouns):   carpet, aircraft, grass, tiger

    Ideas (abstract nouns):   happiness, pride, integrity, discrimination

- Many proper nouns, and some common nouns, are *compound nouns* because they are made up of more than one word.

    Compound proper nouns have two or more capitalized words:

    One person: Martin Luther King

    One place: Fort Worth

    One thing: Golden Gate Bridge

    Compound common nouns may be spelled as one word, as two or more words, or as a hyphenated word:

    One word: football

    Two words: parking lot

    Hyphenated word: brother-in-law

- Nouns that stand for a group are called *collective nouns*. Some examples of collective nouns are *jury, audience,* and *faculty.*

IDENTIFYING NOUNS BY THEIR FEATURES

The definition of a noun does have certain weaknesses. It is important that we determine that certain words name persons, places, things, or ideas and are therefore nouns.

Here are some tests for finding a noun:

- Words that have a plural ending in *s* are definitely nouns. This does not apply to other parts of speech.

  The *helicopter* was late. (singular = one)

  The *helicopters* were late. (plural = more than one)

- Articles (*a, an, the*) are important noun indicators. When they are modifiers (describers), they modify nouns and provide a rough test for words with no plural or with plurals not ending in *s* or *es*.

- The possessive and demonstrative adjectives (*my, our, your, his, their, this, these, such, some, several,* and so on) are important noun indicators. When they are modifiers, they modify nouns and provide a rough test for words with no plural or with plurals not ending in *s* or *es*.

- Word order is sometimes a major clue in the recognition of nouns:

  He trains *seals*. (*Trains* is used as a verb; *seals* is used as a noun.)

  He seals *trains*. (*Seals* is used as a verb; *trains* is used as a noun.)

- Nouns may be recognized by noun suffixes:

Suffix	Examples
-ment	resentment, employment
-ness	goodness, hardness
-er	helper, employer
-ity	conformity, purity
-or	inventor, transgressor
-ance, -ence	endurance, permanence
-ure	pressure, failure
-al	approval, survival
-ion, -tion, -sion	reunion, imagination, decision
-ism	criticism, racism

✌ EXERCISE 1.1 ❧

Determine whether each of the following nouns names a person, place, thing, or idea. Then identify each noun as either a concrete or an abstract noun.

	Person, place, thing, or idea?	Concrete or abstract?
1. street	_____	_____
2. love	_____	_____
3. loneliness	_____	_____
4. loyalty	_____	_____
5. lamp	_____	_____
6. patriotism	_____	_____
7. patio	_____	_____
8. integrity	_____	_____
9. librarian	_____	_____
10. hostess	_____	_____

✌ EXERCISE 1.2 ❧

*Fill the blank in each sentence with an appropriate noun. Then, in the blank to the left of the sentence, indicate what the noun names. Write **P** for person, **PL** for place, **T** for thing, or **I** for idea.*

_____ **1.** Men who fought at the Alamo are known for their _____.

_____ **2.** Mr. Vitatow enjoys visiting the _____.

_____ **3.** There are several beautiful _____ in Paris, France.

_____ **4.** The three soldiers left the _____ at dawn and returned at dusk.

_____ **5.** Her _____ was on the best-seller list for two months.

_____ **6.** The _____ were donated by our members.

_____ **7.** Loyalty, _____, and dependability are important personal attributes.

_____ **8.** The _____ were tuned, and the musicians sat attentively in their seats.

_____ **9.** That _____ looks beautiful on the showroom floor.

_____ **10.** My little _____ likes to bask in the sun.

❧ EXERCISE 1.3 ❧

Compose 10 sentences about your favorite pastime or hobby. Underline the nouns in each sentence.

1. _____

_____

2. _____

_____

3. _____

_____

4. _____

_____

5. _____

_____

6. _____

_____

7. _____

_____

8. _____

_____

9. _____

_____

10. _____

_____

❧ EXERCISE 1.4 ❧

*Identify each noun as either a proper noun (**P**) or a common noun (**C**). Circle any letters that should be capitalized.*

_____ 1. ambulance

_____ 2. general electric company

_____ 3. foyer

_____ 4. will rogers coliseum

_____ 5. dr. henry

_____ 6. corridor

_____ 7. attorney

_____ 8. binoculars

_____ 9. denver, colorado

_____ 10. dallas cowboys (football team)

❧ EXERCISE 1.5 ❧

*Underline the nouns in the following sentences. Above each sentence, identify each noun as either a common noun (**C**) or a proper noun (**P**). Circle any letters that should be capitalized.*

1. The women dress in fine linen, silk, cotton, and velvet.
2. My brother julio scurried hurriedly into the bathroom.
3. Cowboys were riding horses into the sunset.
4. A deep, gruff voice screamed loudly.
5. Many farmers consider the fox a pest and a danger.
6. When mr. Lane interviewed her on wednesday, he asked her to come back on friday.
7. Dr. yakimoto retired last spring to pursue a career in golf.
8. The nurse stuck faranak with a needle.
9. We went to the amon carter museum last May.
10. Chemists must be very careful when they handle dangerous chemicals.

FORMING THE PLURAL OF NOUNS

Nouns are inflected to show singular or plural number. Many people do not remember all spelling rules; therefore, a good source in finding the correct spelling of words is the dictionary.

- Most nouns form the plural by adding *s* to the singular form:

Singular	Plural
missile	missiles
pet	pets

- Nouns ending in *ch*, *sh*, *z*, *x*, and *s* form the plural by adding *-es* to the singular form:

Singular	Plural
branch	branches
box	boxes

- Nouns ending in *y* preceded by a consonant usually change *y* to *i* before adding *-es*:

Singular	Plural
lady	ladies
colony	colonies

- Nouns ending in *y* preceded by a vowel usually add *-s* without changing the final *y*:

Singular	Plural
day	days
chimney	chimneys

- Certain nouns ending in *f* or *fe* change the *f* to *v* before adding the plural ending:

Singular	Plural
hoof	hooves
knife	knives
scarf	scarves

- Certain nouns ending in *f* or *fe* do not change the *f* to *v* before adding the plural ending:

Singular	Plural
chief	chief**s**
safe	safe**s**
gulf	gulf**s**

- Nouns ending in *o* preceded by a vowel add -*s* to the singular to form the plural:

Singular	Plural
radio	radio**s**
cameo	cameo**s**

- Certain nouns ending in *o* preceded by a consonant form their plural by adding -*es* to the singular form. Other nouns ending in *o* preceded by a consonant add -*s* to form the plural.

Singular	Plural
potato	potato**es**
piano	piano**s**

- Certain nouns ending in *o* have more than one acceptable plural form. The more common plural is given first.

Singular	Plural
mosquito	mosquito**es**, mosquito**s**
tornado	tornado**es**, tornado**s**

- A very few nouns form their plural with the -*en* suffix, either with or without additional spelling changes. This plural formation is a remnant from Old English and is exceedingly rare.

Singular	Plural
ox	ox**en**
child	child**ren**
brother	bre**t**h**ren**

- Certain nouns form their plural with an internal change. The plural is formed by changing the root vowel rather than by adding *-s*.

Singular	Plural
man	m**en**
foot	f**ee**t
goose	g**ee**se

- Some nouns borrowed from other languages retain their foreign plurals:

Singular	Plural
alumna	alumn**ae**
alumnus	alumn**i**
schema	schema**ta**
memorandum	memorand**a**
phenomenon	phenomen**a**
thesis	thes**es**
cherub	cherub**im**
phalanx	phalan**ges**

- Certain nouns have the same form for both singular and plural:

Singular	Plural
fish	fish
deer	deer

- Certain compound nouns form their plural by adding *-s* to the main word:

Singular	Plural
attorney general	attorney**s** general
sister-in-law	sister**s**-in-law
runner-up	runner**s**-up
maid of honor	maid**s** of honor
senator-elect	senator**s**-elect

Note that only *count* nouns—nouns that name things that can be counted—have a plural form. *Noncount* nouns—nouns that name things that *cannot* be counted—exist only in the singular form. Examples of noncount nouns that have no plural are *anger, milk,* and *honesty*.

*Underline the correct singular or plural form for each of the nouns in parentheses. Write **S** for singular or **P** for plural in the space provided.*

_____ 1. Tran and Santy are (brother-in-laws, brothers-in-law).

_____ 2. The barber ordered a new shipment of (razor, razors) on Friday.

_____ 3. (Runner-up, Runners-up) will receive $500 scholarships.

_____ 4. We bought a (radio, radios) during the holidays.

_____ 5. Five (governor-elects, governors-elect) attended the conference.

_____ 6. My workout (session, sessions) was fantastic.

_____ 7. The (man, men) waved the flags lazily back and forth as they passed.

_____ 8. Leo's restaurant serves (trout, trouts) on Thursdays.

_____ 9. Mr. Graves sells reconditioned (television, televisions) once a month.

_____ 10. My (sister-in-law, sisters-in-law) has a great personality.

NOUNS AS SUBJECTS

Nouns may be used as subjects of sentences. The word *noun* designates a *class* of English words, but the word *subject* refers to a *function*—how the word is used in a sentence. The *subject* is the main actor in a sentence—the doer of the action or the focus of the verb. Many times the subject is a noun (the name of a person, place, thing, or idea). However, it may be a pronoun (a word that substitutes for a noun). Examples of pronouns are *he, she, it, we, you, they,* and *their.* (For more on pronouns, see Chapter 2.) Most sentences contain a *simple subject* or a *complete subject.* The *simple subject* is an individual word that identifies *who* or *what* did or is or has done to it whatever the sentence asserts. In other words, the *subject* is the word indicating the *topic* of the sentence, telling who or what the sentence is about. The *complete subject* is the simple subject plus any words or phrases that describe or modify it. A *modifier* is a word or group of words that describe a noun or pronoun, telling which one or what kind. The articles *a, an,* and *the* are modifiers, so are adjectives and adverbs. (For more on modifiers, see Chapter 7.)

Simple subject:	The *firefighters* at Station 3 rushed to the firetruck and took off.
Complete subject:	*The firefighters at Station 3* rushed to the firetruck and took off.

☙ EXERCISE 1.7 ❧

Underline the simple subject in each of the following sentences.

1. The sunlight faded the beautiful sofa.
2. The essay was universally accepted.
3. Le'Aisha played the piano like a professional.
4. The question was answered expeditiously.
5. Ashley exercises daily for total physical fitness.
6. Brunches are served at the Remington Hotel on Sundays.
7. Determination is the key to success in this competitive society.
8. Destiny's Child appeared on national television in January.
9. Teachers should practice what they teach.
10. Dinosaurs are extinct reptiles.

Nouns can also serve as *objects*, receiving the action of the verb or, even more often, as the object of a preposition in a prepositional phrase. A *prepositional phrase* is a group of words containing a preposition and its object (a noun or pronoun). *On the table, under the bridge,* and *to him* are prepositional phrases. (Some prepositions are made up of more than one word, such as *in front of*.) The preposition is always the first word in a prepositional phrase, and the noun or pronoun is always the last word. (For more on prepositions, see Chapter 8.)

If you are having trouble identifying the subject of a sentence, it will help if you cross out or mark off all the prepositional phrases. It should then be easy to determine the subject from the nouns or pronouns that remain:

The firefighters ~~at Station 3~~ rushed ~~to the firetruck~~ and took off.

✣ EXERCISE 1.8 ✣

*In each of the following sentences, put parentheses around the prepositional phrases. Underline the complete subject, and write **S** above the simple subject.*

1. A cream-colored cloth in the buffet will cover the Kwanzaa table.
2. The handsome man disappeared into the night.
3. Crystal chandeliers lit up the entire ballroom in the new building.
4. The snow-capped mountains in the distance were simply gorgeous.
5. Rabid rabbits were discovered in the affluent neighborhood.
6. The cries of the newborn baby echoed throughout the house.
7. Violent thunderstorms near the Glenview area frightened the residents.
8. High-pitched screams in the distance led us to the culprit.
9. Calls within the New York area are discounted 5 percent.
10. Rusty copper piping under the sink caused the water contamination.

✣ EXERCISE 1.9 ✣

Underline the nouns in the following selection.

The *Mona Lisa* is known as one of the most admired and famous paintings in the world. In fact, it is so famous that it has been copied millions of times. It was even stolen from the Salon Carré in the Louvre museum in Paris, France. It was rediscovered two years later in a hotel in Florence, Italy. The masterpiece was painted in the 1500s by the great Leonardo da Vinci. It completely mesmerizes its viewers. This painting, which some experts believe depicts a young Florentine woman, is extremely intriguing because the viewer is unable to discern the meaning of the enigmatic smile on her sweet face. When one looks at the *Mona Lisa* from one vantage point, there appears to be a look of sadness or despair on her face. But when viewed from another vantage point, she appears to be mocking the viewer. Even more remarkable, no matter where one stands, her gaze seems direct. If one moves to the right, it appears that her eyes follow; if one moves to the left, it also appears that they follow. In fact, the painting is so intriguing that much study has been devoted to Leonardo's great masterpiece. Some people claim that the picture is actually a portrait of Leonardo himself, posing as a woman. The world will probably never know the secret of the *Mona Lisa*.

2

Pronouns

UNDERSTANDING PRONOUNS

One way to refer to something is to use the noun that names it. It is usually necessary to do this to make clear what you mean. However, once you make clear the identity of the person or thing you are talking about, you can make references without having to give the name each time by using pronouns. In this chapter, you will learn to identify pronouns through their definitions, their classifications, and the features that distinguish them from other parts of speech.

DEFINING PRONOUNS

A *pronoun* is a word that takes the place of a noun.

We looked at the *Mercedes* and were impressed by *it*. (The pronoun *it* stands for *Mercedes*.)

The *manager* suddenly realized that *she* had lost her keys. (The pronoun *she* stands for *manager*.)

Jonathan bragged that *he* was the coolest guy in the class. (The pronoun *he* stands for *Jonathan*.)

It would be awkward to repeat the nouns in these sentences. Pronouns convey the same meaning more efficiently by simply taking the places of the nouns.

IDENTIFYING PRONOUNS BY THEIR FEATURES

Three features distinguish pronouns from other parts of speech.

1. A pronoun, like a noun, may be singular or plural.
2. The form of a pronoun depends on its function in a sentence. Personal pronouns have both subjective and objective forms.
3. Pronouns may show gender. Some singular personal pronouns are masculine, feminine, or neuter.

CLASSIFYING PRONOUNS

There are six types of pronouns: *personal, interrogative, demonstrative, possessive, reflexive,* and *indefinite*.

PERSONAL PRONOUNS

The *personal pronouns* refer to people; the third-person personal pronouns can also refer to places, things, or ideas.

	Nominative or Subjective Case		Objective Case		Possessive Case	
	Singular	*Plural*	*Singular*	*Plural*	*Singular*	*Plural*
First person	I	we	me	us	my, mine	our, ours
Second person	you	you	you	you	your, yours	your, yours
Third person	he	they	him	them	his, her	their, theirs
	she	who	her	whom	hers, its	whose
	it		it		whose	
			whom			

- Using the *first* person, the writer can talk about himself or herself.
- Using the *second* person, the writer can talk about the person or persons to whom he or she is speaking directly.
- Using the *third* person, the writer can talk about anyone or anything else.

18

✣ EXERCISE 2.1 ✣

Underline the 20 personal pronouns in the following sentences.

1. It is not my fault; it is yours.
2. Your property is parallel to mine.
3. Duy decided that he would not keep the appointment.
4. You promised me that you would bake a cake for me.
5. You are to blame for all of the problems.
6. We overcame many obstacles along our way.
7. He came to the church just as he was.
8. All of her worldly possessions were confiscated.
9. He promised to respond as soon as he received the e-mail.
10. McKinsey purchased her shoes in Italy.

✣ EXERCISE 2.2 ✣

Underline the 25 personal pronouns in the following sentences.

1. The newscaster reported the news in his city, and then he collapsed.
2. Most salespeople talk their heads off if you will listen to them.
3. The clown stood on his head for several minutes, and he was not dizzy when he returned to his upright position.
4. Our counselor never advises her students on their career choices.
5. The reporter gave the article to them.
6. If I had a choice, I would not accompany you anywhere.
7. You and your sister are absolutely ridiculous.
8. Her baby boy sucked his fingers until they wrinkled.
9. The report was placed on his desk, but he did not see it.
10. The choice is mine.

❧ EXERCISE 2.3 ❧

Fill each blank with an appropriate personal pronoun.

Malcolm's biggest problem is that _____ is self-centered. _____ never considers the feelings of others. _____ point of view is that _____ agenda is the only one that is important. _____ never gives others the opportunity to do what _____ want to do. Bossing everyone is _____ favorite thing to do. It is _____ way or no way.

❧ EXERCISE 2.4 ❧

Fill each blank with an appropriate personal pronoun.

My friends and _____ took an advanced literature class last spring. _____ was a highly challenging course. _____ were required to read nine novels and to write five essays. What is more, _____ graded _____ own papers. Even though the course was one of the most difficult ones that _____ had ever taken, its areas of concentration proved to be very beneficial to _____.

❧ EXERCISE 2.5 ❧

Fill each blank with an appropriate personal pronoun.

1. That piece of cake is _____, and I will not let anyone else have it.
2. _____ two have been neighbors since childhood.
3. Finally, this is _____ opportunity to make amends for what I did.
4. They have _____ opinion, and we have _____.
5. _____ mother told me that she and Hamid were engaged.

INTERROGATIVE PRONOUNS

Interrogative pronouns are used to form questions to elicit specific information. The following words are interrogative pronouns:

who   whose   whom   which   what

Who was responsible for paying the bill?

Whose sunglasses are these?

To *whom* is this addressed?

Which chicken laid the big egg?

What is the problem with your vacuum cleaner?

✺ EXERCISE 2.6 ✺

Fill each blank with an interrogative pronoun that makes sense.

1. _____ threw the paper in the backyard?

2. _____ article is required for reading?

3. _____ pie was selected to win the blue ribbon?

4. _____ question did he say was silly to ask?

5. _____ did you think I would do?

6. _____ said that airplane pilots should not carry guns?

7. For _____ did you bake the coconut cake?

8. _____ will take the brunt of the complaints?

9. _____ piece of machinery is required to complete the project?

10. To _____ will you award the scholarship?

DEMONSTRATIVE PRONOUNS

Demonstrative pronouns refer to specific persons or things without naming them. The following words are demonstrative pronouns:

this   that   these   those

When you use demonstratives in speech, you often actually point at the objects you are talking about.

This is the one I want.

Look at *that*.

These are the ones I am referring to.

She will clean *those* later.

ᔓ EXERCISE 2.7 ᔔ

Fill each blank with a demonstrative pronoun that makes sense.

1. _____ are not the tapes that I ordered.
2. _____ is the broken computer.
3. _____ is the thermostat on which they changed the temperature.
4. _____ is about all I can take.
5. _____ are the people who live next door.
6. _____ is a precarious situation.
7. _____ gives me a start every time I walk into the room.
8. _____ was a terrifying movie for a child to view.
9. _____ are my snowshoes in the garage.
10. _____ are made from quality material.

POSSESSIVE PRONOUNS

Possessive pronouns show ownership. Unlike possessive nouns, they do not require apostrophes.

That ballpoint pen is *yours* to keep.

Hers was the affidavit they submitted.

Our organization tripled the scholarship fund this year.

❧ *EXERCISE 2.8* ❧

Underline the correct possessive pronoun in each of the following sentences.

1. This is (yours, your) opportunity to make a good impression on the new teacher.
2. (Who, Whose) eyeglasses are these?
3. It is (yours, your), not mine.
4. (Who, Whose) house is the blue one with a white picket fence at the top of the hill?
5. (It, Its) focus is movie production.
6. (Your, Yours) mother was clearly enchanted with the beautiful present you gave her.
7. (Their, They) opinion means a great deal to me.
8. No one in this room has seen (she, her) missing bookbag.
9. Humans have always been fascinated by the moon and (it, its) mystery.
10. (They, Their) caricatures are featured in the daily paper.

REFLEXIVE PRONOUNS

Pronouns ending in *-self* or *-selves* are called reflexive pronouns. A *reflexive pronoun* directs the action of the verb back on the subject of the sentence.

My son hurt *himself* playing soccer.

	Antecedent	Reflexive Pronoun
Singular	I	myself
	you	yourself
	he	himself (*never* hisself)
	she	herself
	it	itself
Plural	we	ourselves
	you	yourselves
	they	themselves (*never* theirselves)

☙ EXERCISE 2.9 ❧

Fill each blank with the appropriate reflexive pronoun.

1. I sewed a beautiful dress for _____.
2. After a while, the supervisor _____ became suspicious of the new employee.
3. You should be proud of _____.
4. The children _____ broke all of the ancient artifacts.
5. She did _____ a favor and resigned.
6. Monica _____ was prepared for the outcome.
7. They patted _____ on their backs.
8. We _____ should make restitution for cheating them out of their land.
9. The little kitten _____ bounced the ball to me.
10. You should give _____ credit for discovering the error.

Fill each blank with an appropriate reflexive pronoun.

1. He told _____ that things would get better soon.
2. We gave _____ huge raises even though the yearly profit was down.
3. Ask _____ if your decision was feasible.
4. Michael prided _____ on being the first person to receive the award.
5. Elizabeth revealed _____ after a long period of silence.
6. They treated _____ to fabulous makeovers.
7. I think that I owe it to _____ to have a good time.
8. If history repeats _____, the stock market will rise again.
9. He unraveled the cord _____.
10. Linda gave _____ three weeks to complete the project.

PRONOUN AGREEMENT

A pronoun must agree with (match) the noun or pronoun it refers to in number (singular or plural). If the pronoun is singular, it must also agree in gender (masculine or feminine). The word that the pronoun refers to is called the *antecedent*. Some nouns may be either *masculine* or *feminine;* others, called *common-gender nouns,* can be both. If a common-gender noun can be both masculine and feminine in a particular sentence, use pronouns that reflect both genders (*his or her,* for example). If a noun is neither masculine nor feminine, it is *neuter* and requires a neuter pronoun. *It* and *its* are neuter pronouns.

J.T. and Flora lived in *their* house for more than 30 years. (*Their* agrees with *J.T. and Flora* because two or more antecedents joined by *and* are plural.)

Flora still lives in *her* house. (*Her* agrees with *Flora* because both are singular and feminine.)

Each *architect* completed *his or her* drawing in the time allotted. (The gender of each architect is not specified; therefore, the expression *his or her* is used.)

The *butterfly* flew into the well and got *its* wings wet. (*Butterfly* is a neuter noun; therefore, it requires the neuter pronoun *its.*)

A pronoun is italicized in each of the following sentences. Underline its antecedent.

1. Marcia practiced *her* piano lesson for six hours.
2. The doctors schedule *their* appointments in the afternoon.
3. Investors pooled *their* resources to open a new firm.
4. Joan canceled *her* appointment with the gastroenterologist.
5. Demetrice eats pizza with *her* co-workers every Friday.
6. After scoring a touchdown, Henry fell to *his* knees and let out a whoop.
7. Frantic motorists waited in *their* cars.
8. The injured bird lay on *its* back and died.
9. The actor sold *his* mansion for an estimated $10 million.
10. The little puppy stood on *its* hind legs and begged for food.

PRONOUNS WITH COLLECTIVE NOUNS

Collective nouns represent a group that acts as a single whole. The following are some commonly used collective nouns:

board	company	group	public
class	crowd	jury	scissors
college	faculty	orchestra	society
committee	family	panel	team

Collective nouns may be singular or plural, depending on whether the writer is describing the group as a unit or the individual members of the group. Therefore, the pronoun used to refer to the collective noun may be singular or plural in a particular context.

The *jury* reached *its* decision based on strong circumstantial evidence. (Even though a jury is composed of several members, it acts as one unit. Therefore, the antecedent *jury* takes the singular pronoun *its*.)

The *board* voted to award *themselves* a bonus. (Each person on the board would receive a bonus, not the board itself, so the antecedent *board* in this sentence takes the reflexive pronoun *themselves*.)

INDEFINITE PRONOUNS

An *indefinite pronoun* does not refer to a specific person, place, or thing. Most indefinite pronouns are singular and require singular verbs. However, there are some indefinite pronouns that are always plural and some that take a singular or plural verb depending on the meaning in the sentence.

- The following constructions are singular; therefore, the pronouns that refer to them must also be singular:

  each (of)   either (of)   neither (of)   one (of)

When these pronouns are used with *of*, *of* introduces a prepositional phrase (see Chapter 8). To select a pronoun to match the antecedent, cross out the prepositional phrase, but note the gender of the noun serving as the object of the preposition in it. There may be modifiers (describers) in the middle of the prepositional phrase.

Neither of the two men paid for *his* ticket. (*Of the two men* is a prepositional phrase, and *men* is masculine. The subject is *neither*, which is singular. Therefore, the singular masculine pronoun *his* is required.)

Each of the jewels has *its* special brilliance. (*Of the jewels* is a prepositional phrase, and *jewels* is neuter. The subject is *each*, which is singular. Therefore, the singular neuter pronoun *its* is required.)

Either of the accountants may submit *his or her* bid. (*Of the accountants* is a prepositional phrase, and *accountants* is a common-gender noun. The subject is *either*, which is singular. Therefore, the expression *his or her* is required.)

Fill each blank with an appropriate pronoun, and underline its antecedent. Make sure each pronoun agrees in number and gender with its antecedent.

1. One of the cottages has _____ own character.
2. Every one of the kittens had a white spot on _____ back.
3. Either of these televisions will work if _____ has time to warm up.
4. Neither of the contractors wanted _____ products displayed.
5. Everyone has done _____ work properly.
6. Neither of the artists showed _____ painting.
7. Each of the scholars wanted credit for _____ work.
8. Every one of the contest winners accepted _____ prize graciously.
9. Neither of them was present when _____ name was called.
10. Every one of the clowns put on _____ makeup before the crowd arrived.

- The following indefinite pronouns are always singular, though students often process them as plural:

another	everyone	no one
anybody	everything	nothing
anything	much (of)	one (of)
each (of)	neither (of)	somebody
either (of)	nobody	someone
everybody	none (of)	something

Examine the following sentence:

Everyone has *their* own thoughts concerning the situation.

Although to some people this sentence makes *logical* sense, it is *grammatically* incorrect. Because *everyone* is an indefinite pronoun that is always singular, the sentence should be written as follows:

Everyone has *his or her* own thoughts concerning the situation.

Some writers might prefer to rewrite the sentence to avoid the awkward use of *his or her.*

- The following indefinite pronouns are always plural:

  both   few   many   others   several

  Both of the girls *are* very funny.
  Several of the authors *plan* to participate in the extravaganza.

- The following indefinite pronouns take either a singular or a plural verb, depending on the meaning in the sentence:

  any   all   more   most   none   some

  Some was spilled. (singular)
  Some were yellow roses. (plural)

❧ EXERCISE 2.13 ❧

Underline the verb form that agrees with the pronoun in each of the following sentences.

1. Several (succeed, succeeds) despite their obstacles.
2. Some milk (was, were) set aside for the kitten.
3. Neither of you (cause, causes) the problem.
4. No one (know, knows) the trouble we experience.
5. Will anyone (come, comes) to Annie's rescue?
6. Nothing (seem, seems) concrete at this point.
7. Everybody (scream, screams) during horror movies.
8. In this recession, few (plan, plans) to invest in the stock market.
9. Many will (abide, abides) by the rules even when they do not have to.
10. Some (was, were) high-priced items.

PRONOUNS USED AS SUBJECTS AND AS OBJECTS

The *subjective forms* of personal pronouns (sometimes called *nominative case*) are as follows:

Singular	Plural
I	we
you	you
he, she, it	they

Use the subjective form of a pronoun whenever the pronoun is the subject of a verb. A verb (see Chapter 3) is a word that shows action, like *swim* or *run*. A verb may also show state of being, as is the case with *is, am, was,* and *were*. Certain verbs are *linking verbs*, including *feel, appear, taste, smell, look,* and *sound*.

In the following sentences, subject pronouns do the acting:

I hope to see you soon.
We devised a plan of escape.
He and *she* are acclaimed journalists.

Object pronouns receive the action. The *objective form* of the personal pronoun is called the *objective case*.

Singular	Plural
me	us
you	you
him, her, it	them

- Use the objective form of the personal pronoun when the pronoun is the direct object of the verb:

    Husham defended *her*.

- Use the objective form of the personal pronoun when the pronoun is the indirect object of the verb:

    Chen Ho gave *him* a new weed eater.

- Use the objective form of a personal pronoun when the pronoun is the object of a preposition:

    This is between *him* and *me*.

Selecting the correct pronoun for a sentence becomes confusing when more than one person is mentioned. To figure out the correct pronoun, temporarily remove the other person from the sentence.

Problem: Vic and (me, I) stayed up all night.

Steps:
1. Remove Vic from the sentence.
2. Now, would you say "*Me* stayed up all night" or "*I* stayed up all night"?
3. You would say *I.* So the correct expression would be *Vic and I.*

Solution: Vic and *I* stayed up all night.

Problem: Jonathan plans to go fishing with Jeff and (me, I).

Steps:
1. Remove *Jeff* from the sentence.
2. Would you say "Jonathan plans to go fishing with *I*" or "Jonathan plans to go fishing with *me*"?
3. You would say *me.* So the correct expression would be *with Jeff and me.*

Solution: Jonathan plans to go fishing with Jeff and *me.*

EXERCISE 2.14

Underline the pronouns used as subjects in the following sentences.

1. <u>He</u> sprinkled a dash of red pepper on his pizza.
2. <u>She</u> expounded on controversial news issues.
3. <u>He</u> was hit by an 18-wheeler while he was walking home.
4. <u>I</u> sit around the pool every afternoon and daydream.
5. Rod and <u>I</u> ran in the fall marathon.
6. Yvonne and <u>I</u> shoveled the snow.
7. <u>He</u> passed the test with flying colors.
8. <u>We</u> cared little about what she thought.
9. <u>They</u> told a story that fooled everyone.
10. <u>He</u> screamed when he won the grand prize.

EXERCISE 2.15

Underline the correct compound pronouns in each sentence.

1. Why not give those banquet tickets to (him and her, him and she)?
2. Those poems they read at the ceremony were written for (him and her, him and she).
3. Besides (you and I, you and me), no one knows the secret.
4. Between (you and I, you and me), I don't think he has a chance of winning the gold medal.
5. You walked near (him and her, he and her).
6. Don't ask (her, she) to baby-sit.
7. The supervisor gave too much work to (we, us) overworked employees.
8. Both of his brothers want to be just like (he, him).
9. (You and I, You and me) have been friends for ages.
10. That vase was a wedding present from (they, them) to (us, we).

Look for pronouns as you read a newspaper or magazine. Find an article that contains as many examples as possible of pronouns that were discussed in this chapter. On a sheet of paper, categorize the pronouns.

THE USE OF *WHO* AND *WHOM*

Choosing between *who* and *whom* is a problem for many writers. *Who* is the subjective (nominative) form; *whom* is the objective form. Similarly, *whoever* is the subjective form; *whomever* is the objective form.

Problem: Tierra was the girl (who, whom) welcomed the audience.
Steps:
   1. Focus on the clause containing *who* or *whom: (who, whom) welcomed the audience.*
   2. Identify the verb: *welcomed.*
   3. Is *who* the subject of the verb? If so, the nominative case is correct.
   4. The nominative case form is *who.*
Solution: Tierra was the girl *who* welcomed the audience.

Problem: Do you know (who, whom) she is?
Steps:
   1. The *who* clause is *(who, whom) she is.*
   2. The verb in the clause is *is,* a linking verb (see Chapter 3), which by definition always links two nominatives.
   3. Is *who* the subject of the verb? No, it is the *predicate nominative,* linked to the subject by the verb *is.*
   4. The nominative case form is *who.*
Solution: Do you know *who* she is?

Problem: I hired Precious, (who, whom) my friends recommended.

Steps:

1. The *who* clause is *(who, whom) my friends recommended.*
2. The verb in the clause is *recommended.*
3. Is *who* the subject of the verb? No, the subject is *friends.* The pronoun is the *object* of the verb: *my friends recommended (who, whom).* The objective case is therefore required.
4. The objective form is *whom.*

Solution: I hired Precious, *whom* my friends recommended.

Problem: Virgetta, (who, whom) I sat next to, introduced the speaker.

Steps:

1. The *who* clause is *(who, whom) I sat next to.*
2. The verb in the clause is *sat.*
3. Is *who* the subject of the verb? No, the subject is *I.* The pronoun is the *object* of the preposition *next to: I sat next to (who, whom).* The objective case is therefore required.
4. The objective form is *whom.*

Solution: Virgetta, *whom* I sat next to, introduced the speaker.

WHOEVER AND WHOMEVER

Choosing between *whoever* and *whomever* is a problem for many writers. *Whoever* is the subjective (nominative) form; *whomever* is the objective form. Disregard all the words in the sentence that come before *whoever* or *whomever*. Substitute *he* or *him* for *whoever* or *whomever*. If *he* makes sense, the answer is *whoever*. If *him* makes sense, the answer is *whomever*.

Problem: Give the grand prize to (whoever, whomever) pulls the lucky number.

Steps:

1. Disregard all the words in the sentence that come before *whoever* or *whomever*. Therefore, disregard *Give the grand prize to.*

2. Substitute *he* or *him*. Would you say *he* or *him pulls the lucky number*? You would say *he pulls the lucky number*.

3. *He* is the nominative form, so the correct word is *whoever*.

Solution: Give the grand prize to *whoever* pulls the lucky number.

Problem: Give the ticket to (whoever, whomever) you please.

Steps:

1. Disregard all the words in the sentence that come before *whoever* or *whomever*. Therefore, disregard *Give the ticket to.*

2. Substitute *he* or *him*. Would you say *you please he* or *you please him*? You would say *you please him.*

3. *Him* is in the objective case, so the correct word is *whomever*.

Solution: Give the ticket to *whomever* you please.

✥ EXERCISE 2.17 ✥

Underline the correct pronoun in each sentence.

1. Malcolm is the one (who, whom) is responsible for the error.
2. (Who, Whom) will pick up the author at the airport this evening?
3. We will give the Trailblazer Award to (whoever, whomever) deserves it.
4. (Whoever, Whomever) is present will receive the brunt of the accusations.
5. The manager rewarded the person (who, whom) he hired last.
6. Hand one to (whoever, whomever) you see.
7. (Who, Whom) does he think will support his actions?
8. (Whoever, Whomever) is the highest bidder will get the baby grand piano.
9. The award will go to (whoever, whomever) the judges choose.
10. (Whoever, Whomever) did this should suffer the consequences.

Underline the correct pronoun in each sentence.

1. For (who, whom) were the unkind remarks intended?
2. (Who, Whom) is the person that Bell South gave a 30 percent discount to for averaging $200 or more on long-distance phone calls.
3. I will select (whoever, whomever) you suggest.
4. To (who, whom) is this postcard addressed?
5. The beautiful flowers were intended for (whoever, whomever) completed his or her work first.
6. Margene is the contestant (who, whom) the judges selected.
7. (Who, Whom) is the young man wearing the Rolex watch?
8. (Whoever, Whomever) the bonus check was left for is no concern of mine.
9. From (who, whom) did you get this gorgeous necklace?
10. (Who, Whom) will help me decorate the grand ballroom?

❧ 3 ❧

Regular and Irregular Verbs

UNDERSTANDING VERBS

Every complete sentence contains at least one verb. Effective use of verbs can communicate the emotion, thought, or action that is the essence of good writing. In Chapters 3, 4, and 5, you will study verbs by learning to recognize them through their definition, the classes into which they can be grouped, and the features that distinguish them from other parts of speech.

DEFINING VERBS

A *verb* is a word that shows action (for example, *swim, run, talk*), indicates a state of being (*is, become, seem, appear*), or conveys a perception through the senses (*smell, sound, taste, look*). A verb tells *what the subject does* or *what is done to the subject*. A complete sentence always contains a verb.

IDENTIFYING VERBS BY THEIR FUNCTION

When you can identify the verb in a sentence, you can easily detect the rest of the parts of the sentence. Here are two tests for identifying the verb in a sentence:

1. Ask what the sentence *says about the subject*.

   The ship docked.

   What does the sentence say about the ship? The ship *docked. Docked* is the verb.

2. Put *I, you, she, it,* or *they* in front of the word you think is a verb. If the result makes sense, the word is a verb.

Verbs do the following things:

Make statements: The graduation ceremony *lasted* four hours.

Make requests: Please *bring* my notebook to the meeting Friday.

Ask questions: What *started* the disagreement among the employees?

Give commands: *Send* the answers to the test questions to me immediately.

𝒥 EXERCISE 3.1 ❧

Identify each of the following sentences either as a statement, a request, a question, or a command.
In the blank, write S for statement, R for request, Q for question, or C for command.

_____ **1.** Take English 312 instead of Literature I.

_____ **2.** Albert Einstein paved the way for other scientists.

_____ **3.** Every explanation revealed crystal-clear answers.

_____ **4.** Please contact the entertainment personnel before 5 p.m.

_____ **5.** Criticizing yourself for past errors does not help.

_____ **6.** The light from the lamp beamed brilliantly across the table.

_____ **7.** Didn't I tell you that the truth always prevails?

_____ **8.** Charles Dickens grew up in a family beset by financial insecurity.

_____ **9.** Please leave a message on the recorder in the reception room.

_____ **10.** Do not touch that button without my permission.

CLASSIFYING VERBS

• Most verbs show action, either physical or mental:

The police officer *yelled* loudly during the traffic jam. (physical action)

Shane *thought* of a plan that would work. (mental action)

- Other verbs, known as *linking verbs*, do not show action but rather give information about the state of the subject:

> This book *is* a classic.
> Darnell *seems* tired today.

Because linking verbs express no action, they cannot pass action on to a receiving object. Pronouns used to rename the subject after these verbs must therefore be in the subjective (nominative) case.

> The last ones to leave the house *were* Toby and *I*.

- If the verb in a sentence consists of more than one word in what is known as a *verb phrase*, the last verb of the phrase is the main verb. The other verbs in the phrase are *helping verbs* because they help the main verb express action:

> Cynthia and Trang *will walk* a 10-mile stretch in the marathon. (*Will* is the helping verb. *Walk* is the main verb.)
> You *have seen* the result of disobeying my orders. (*Have* is the helping verb. *Seen* is the main verb.)

Helping verbs include all forms of *be* (*is, am, was, were, are*) as well as some other frequently used verbs:

been	can	should	had
do	could	would	may
does	will	have	might
did	shall	has	must

Sometimes the main verb is separated from helping verbs by words such as *always, usually, never,* and *not*. These words are not considered part of the verb phrase:

> I *will* always *remember* you.
> Cleo *has* never *spoken* an unkind word.
> You *will* not *regret* supporting me in my effort.
> *Did* you ever *think* about what you are doing?

EXERCISE 3.2

Circle the main verb in each sentence and underline the helping verbs.

1. The book may not have been stolen after all.

2. Did you see the film?

3. Has the boy next door been introduced to you?

4. They should certainly be arriving any minute.

5. You may notice the bundle of rods, which are held together by a strap.

6. Do you know how or where you are going?

7. Franklin has observed the experiment for the past three months.

8. Jan's answer will determine the outcome of the annual spelling contest.

9. Carrington has mastered the art of reading for details.

10. Does it make sense to alter your plans at this point?

PRINCIPAL PARTS OF VERBS

Verb *tenses* are the *times* expressed by verbs. English has only two inflected tenses, *past* and *present*. All other verb forms are aspects of either the past or the present. Verbs have four principal parts: *present, past, past participle,* and *present participle.* These parts can be used to build the verb tenses.

Most verbs in English are *regular*, which means that the simple past and the past participle are formed by adding *-d* or *-ed* to the present tense form. The *past participle* is the form of the verb used with the helping verbs *have, has*, and *had*. The *present participle* is the form of the verb used with an *-ing* ending.

Present	Past	Past Participle	Present Participle
work	worked	worked	working
talk	talked	talked	talking
frighten	frightened	frightened	frightening

Identify the verb that goes with the subject of each sentence. Indicate in the blank whether it is in the present or past tense.

_____ **1.** Mary entered the museum through the south door.

_____ **2.** Constance practiced her piano lessons.

_____ **3.** He scrambled through the papers with a horrified look on his face.

_____ **4.** You eat what is placed on the table.

_____ **5.** The VCR sounded loudly throughout the house.

_____ **6.** I assume that you met the requirements for admission.

_____ **7.** Call the honorees one week prior to the luncheon.

_____ **8.** He scribbled his name in the wet cement.

_____ **9.** I park in the empty parking lot next to the garage.

_____ **10.** Tony skipped the last line of the reading.

IRREGULAR VERB FORMS: *BE, HAVE,* AND *DO*

Three of the most common verbs in English—*be, have,* and *do*—are *irregular,* meaning that they have present, past, and participle forms that do not follow the rules for regular verbs.

Forms of *Be*

Singular	**Plural**
Present Tense	
I am	we are
you are	you are
he, she, it is	they are
Past Tense	
I was	we were
you were	you were
he, she, it was	they were

Past Participle: been

Forms of *Have*

	Singular	**Plural**
Present Tense		
	I have	we have
	you have	you have
	he, she, it has	they have

Past Tense: had

Past Participle: had

Forms of *Do*

	Singular	**Plural**
Present Tense		
	I do	we do
	you do	you do
	he, she, it does	they do

Past Tense: did

Past Participle: done

✌ *EXERCISE 3.4* ✌

Underline the correct form of the verb be *in each sentence.*

1. Sounds (is, are) waves in the air.
2. There (is, are) something strange about his reaction to the proposal.
3. The professor (is, are) very impressed with your improvement in foreign language.
4. Ericka (is, are) the only three-year-old girl in the neighborhood who can spell *encyclopedia.*
5. Living things (is, are) made of atoms.
6. A plaque (was, were) presented to Pham at the banquet.
7. You (was, were) present when he slipped on the icy curve.
8. Shawnette (is, are) satisfied with her raise.
9. Madeline (was, were) the recipient of school supplies from the federal government.
10. (Was, Were) you the cause of her dismay?

Underline the correct form of the verb in each sentence.

1. She (has, have) a peculiar way of showing her concern.
2. Evergreens (has, have) leaves especially suited to stand the cold weather.
3. I (has, have) an insatiable desire to eat ice cream.
4. Three guitars and four flutes (was, were) on the piano.
5. It (is, are) difficult for you to distinguish right from wrong.
6. My plans (is, are) not your plans.
7. Procrastinators (has, have) difficulty completing tasks.
8. My sister (has, have) a wonderful sense of humor.
9. (Is, Are) your problem my concern?
10. The girls' ages (is, are) three, five, and seven.

OTHER IRREGULAR VERBS

There are many other irregular verbs in English; the following are the most common.

Present Tense	Past Tense	Past Participle
arise	arose	arisen
awaken	awoke, awaked	awoken, awaked
begin	began	begun
bend	bent	bent
bind	bound	bound
bite	bit	bitten
bleed	bled	bled
blow	blew	blew
break	broke	broken
bring	brought	brought
build	built	built
burn	burned, burnt	burned, burnt
burst	burst	burst

Present Tense	Past Tense	Past Participle
buy	bought	bought
catch	caught	caught
choose	chose	chosen
cling	clung	clung
come	came	come
cost	cost	cost
creep	crept	crept
cut	cut	cut
deal	dealt	dealt
dig	dug	dug
draw	drew	drawn
drink	drank	drunk
drive	drove	driven
eat	ate	eaten
fall	fell	fallen
feed	fed	fed
feel	felt	felt
fight	fought	fought
find	found	found
flee	fled	fled
fling	flung	flung
fly	flew	flown
forbid	forbade	forbidden
forget	forgot	forgotten, forgot
freeze	froze	frozen
get	got	got, gotten
give	gave	given
go	went	gone
grind	ground	ground
grow	grew	grown
hang*	hung	hung

Hang meaning "execute by hanging" is regular.

Present Tense	Past Tense	Past Participle
hear	heard	heard
hide	hid	hidden, hid
hold	held	held
hurt	hurt	hurt
keep	kept	kept
knit	knit, knitted	knit, knitted
know	knew	known
lay	laid	laid
lead	led	led
leap	leaped, leapt	leaped, leapt
leave	left	left
lend	lent	lent
let	let	let
lie	lay	lain
light	lighted, lit	lighted, lit
lose	lost	lost
make	made	made
mean	meant	meant
meet	met	met
mistake	mistook	mistaken
pay	paid	paid
prove	proved	proved, proven
put	put	put
quit	quit	quit
read	read	read
ride	rode	ridden
ring	rang	rung
rise	rose	risen
run	ran	run
say	said	said
see	saw	seen
seek	sought	sought
sell	sold	sold

Present Tense	Past Tense	Past Participle
send	sent	sent
set	set	set
sew	sewed	sewn, sewed
shake	shook	shaken
shine*	shone, shined	shone, shined
shoot	shot	shot
show	showed	shown
shrink	shrank, shrunk	shrunk, shrunken
shut	shut	shut
sing	sang	sung
sit	sat	sat
sleep	slept	slept
slide	slid	slid
sling	slung	slung
sow	sowed	sown, sowed
speak	spoke	spoken
speed	sped, speeded	sped, speeded
spend	spent	spent
spit	spit, spat	spit, spat
spring	sprang, sprung	sprung
stand	stood	stood
steal	stole	stolen
stick	stuck	stuck
sting	stung	stung
stink	stank, stunk	stunk
stride	strode	stridden
strike	struck	struck, stricken
string	strung	strung
strive	strived, strove	striven, strived
swear	swore	sworn
sweat	sweat, sweated	sweat, sweated

Shine meaning "polish" is regular.

Present Tense	Past Tense	Past Participle
swell	swelled	swelled, swollen
swim	swam	swum
swing	swung	swung
take	took	taken
teach	taught	taught
tear	tore	torn
tell	told	told
throw	threw	thrown
understand	understood	understood
wake	woke, waked	woken, waked, woke
wear	wore	worn
weave (make cloth)	wove, weaved	woven, weaved
weep	wept	wept
win	won	won
wind	wound	wound
wring	wrung	wrung
write	wrote	written

❧ EXERCISE 3.6 ❧

Underline the correct form of each irregular verb.

1. Sampson (wrote, written) a letter to Senator Yarborough yesterday.
2. This old coat is (wore, worn) to a frazzle.
3. He (wringed, wrung) the towel thoroughly before he hung it on the bar.
4. I (took, taken) some flu medicine that was three years old.
5. He had (stole, stolen) the expensive overcoat.
6. Simone (throwed, threw) the newspaper furiously.
7. Thai (singed, sang) the song to the beat of the music.
8. I (sweared, swore) that I would never do that again.
9. Mr. Ho (teached, taught) me a lesson that I will never forget.
10. I (tell, tells) the same story every time.

EXERCISE 3.7

Identify the verb that goes with the subject of each sentence. Indicate in the blank whether it is in the present or past tense.

_____ 1. The engineer perfected the mechanical tool.

_____ 2. American Airlines employees schedule flights to meet the needs of the customers.

_____ 3. Glencrest schoolteachers participate in the events at the state fair.

_____ 4. The wind blew ferociously all night.

_____ 5. The handsome man stood at the edge of town prompting newcomers.

_____ 6. The mastermind of the new invention attends Friday meetings.

_____ 7. Tile floors shone when we put a fresh coat of wax on them.

_____ 8. Veronica completed the legal work in approximately ten days.

_____ 9. The wedding party enjoys the fun and frolic.

_____ 10. Most junior colleges changed their names to community colleges.

NONSTANDARD VERB FORMS

Many people use nonstandard forms of verbs in everyday speech. Community dialect is powerful, but it is not acceptable in the academic or business world. Regular English verb forms must be used.

	Nonstandard (Do not use in writing)		Standard (Use in writing)	
Present Tense	I cooks	we cooks	I cook	we cook
	you cooks	you cooks	you cook	you cook
	he, she, it cook	they cooks	he, she, it cooks	they cook
Past Tense	I cook	we cook	I cooked	we cooked
	you cook	you cook	you cooked	you cooked
	he, she, it cook	they cook	he, she, it cooked	they cooked

✌ EXERCISE 3.8 ✌

The following sentences need -s or -es endings added or eliminated. Cross out each nonstandard verb form. Write the standard verb form in the space provided.

1. Lawyers sometimes charges high fees for their advice. _____
2. Time pass rapidly when you are having a good time. _____
3. We walks to school on sunny days. _____
4. It pay to be kind. _____
5. They answers the telephone every time it rings. _____
6. The students works the problem in a few minutes. _____
7. I eats a good breakfast every morning. _____
8. He eat six small meals a day to increase his metabolism. _____
9. She donate large sums of money to the Red Cross. _____
10. You tickles me when you laugh that crazy laugh. _____

✌ EXERCISE 3.9 ✌

Underline the correct verb form in each sentence.

1. It (do, does) tend to rain during spring break.
2. I (swim, swims) every day to build up my stamina.
3. Jeremy (want, wants) his own apartment.
4. Lin (do, does) articulate well.
5. I (feel, feels) good when I eat breakfast in the morning.
6. She (become, becomes) angry when he questions her integrity.
7. He (do, does) ask too many silly questions.
8. The pictures (look, looks) good hanging in the hallway.
9. He (do, does) limit his cholesterol intake.
10. I (has, have) a sneaky suspicion concerning his high grades.

Underline the verb that goes with the subject of each sentence in the following selection.

The man across the street has the worst table manners that I have ever seen! As a kind gesture, Mother invited him to dinner last week. The minute he sat down at the table, the show began. As he ate his corn on the cob, his big, white teeth went clackety-clack like the sound of an old Remington typewriter. Droppings of corn landed on the table. He continued his meal, never noticing anything. He choked when he took a gigantic bite of his baked chicken. Gasping for breath and beating his mammoth chest, his eyes rolled back in his head. Suddenly, the big piece of chicken popped out of his mouth and fell into his overloaded plate. When he had finished his salad, he slurped the juice like a thirsty puppy lapping water. Instead of breaking his bread, he attempted to cut it. It went flying across the dining room. Green beans, clenched tightly between his fingers and thumb, dripped juices as his hands made their way to his mouth. The juices trickled down his chin and landed on the front of his crisp, white shirt before plopping on the immaculately clean velvet chair. His lips lunged in and out as he slurped the iced tea. Then he licked his plate clean, let out a titanic burp, got up from the table, and said that he was headed home. I was glad when the evening ended and hoped that Mother would never invite him again.

Underline the verb that goes with the subject of each sentence in the following selection.

Did anyone ever tell you that you were all wet? That is correct, you know, though perhaps not in the way the remark was intended. For a fundamental fact of life is that our bodies float in water. Every cell that we call our own is constantly bathed in a fluid environment. Scientists refer to this fluid as *internal medium*. In most places in the body, the internal medium is only a film separating each tiny cell from its neighbors. The medium is more than just a screen of water. All the things—food, energy, waste material—that pass into or out of our cells are transmitted in the internal medium. In this way, the fluid serves as the middleman of life, the reservoir connecting our living selves with the outside world.

Although the world around us is a changing place, the human body's internal environment is remarkably unchanging. The body can live where the climate is very hot or where it is very cold, within reasonable limits, of course. The body does well at high altitudes or at altitudes below the level of the sea, again with limits in both directions. A look at the variety of food eaten around the world shows that the body can exist on a wide range of diets. But despite the marked changes in the external environment, the internal environment somehow remains constant. This ability to "roll with the punches" is one of the marvels of the body and explains why we can live almost anywhere on the face of the earth.

❧ 4 ❧

Subject-Verb Agreement

A verb must agree with its subject in number. A *singular subject* (one person or thing) takes a singular verb. A *plural subject* (more than one person or thing) takes a plural verb. Normally, nouns that end in *s* are plural (*boys, teachers*), but verbs that end in *s* are singular (*goes, needs*).

Singular subject/singular verb: The *chemist pours* the solution into the flask with ease.

Plural subject/plural verb: The *chemists pour* the solution into the flask with ease.

❧ EXERCISE 4.1 ❧

*In the blank, write **S** if the word is singular and **P** if the word is plural.*

_____ **1.** practitioner

_____ **2.** sofa

_____ **3.** satellite

_____ **4.** clips

_____ **5.** dentist

_____ **6.** dollars

_____ **7.** article

_____ **8.** magazines

_____ **9.** laminator

_____ **10.** radios

The form of the verb used with the singular pronouns *I* and *you* is regularly the same as the plural form. However, in the third person singular, the agreement in number presents a problem. Note the following:

	Singular	**Plural**
First person	I play	we play
Second person	you play	you play
Third person	he, she, it *plays*	they play

☙ EXERCISE 4.2 ❧

Put a wavy line under the subject in each sentence; then underline the verb that agrees in number with the subject.

1. Police officers (arrive, arrives) just before dawn.
2. You (look, looks) good standing in that doorway.
3. It (give, gives) me great pleasure to see you looking so well.
4. They (read, reads) the newspaper early every morning.
5. Secretly, Mary (watch, watches) him from a distance.
6. Every time she goes onto the hockey field, she (make, makes) history.
7. He (turn, turns) a corner every five minutes.
8. Concrete evidence (is, are) needed to prosecute.
9. Donnie (stand, stands) in line for movie tickets every Saturday night.
10. She never (cease, ceases) to amaze me.

PERSON OF NOUNS

All nouns are third person.

❧ EXERCISE 4.3 ❧

Put a wavy line under the subject in each sentence; then underline the verb that agrees with the subject in person.

1. Marguerite (enjoy, enjoys) dining in the evening.
2. Shaunette (play, plays) the piano very well.
3. The marriage (appear, appears) to be on solid ground.
4. Our justice of the peace (arrive, arrives) at work early and leaves late.
5. The legal documents (prove, proves) to be helpful for verification.
6. The United Way (benefit, benefits) many needy people.
7. Your printer (print, prints) faster than mine does.
8. Jean's statement (appear, appears) inconclusive.
9. This glass marble (am, is) highly collectable.
10. Mercury (have, has) been called quicksilver.

SUBJECT-VERB AGREEMENT ERRORS

Mistakes in subject-verb agreement often occur in the following situations:

1. With compound subjects
2. When a verb comes before the subject
3. With indefinite pronouns
4. When words come between the subject and the verb

COMPOUND SUBJECTS JOINED BY *AND*

- Two or more subjects joined by *and* usually require a plural verb:

    Sonny and Cher *were* great together.

- A *compound subject* thought of as a single unit requires a singular verb:

    Ham and eggs *is* my favorite breakfast.

OTHER COMPOUND SUBJECTS

If compound subjects are joined by *or, nor,* or *not only . . . but also,* problems may arise.

- If both subjects are singular, the verb is singular:

    The professor or the counselor *is* wrong.

- If both subjects are plural, the verb is plural:

    The professors or the counselors *are* wrong.

- If one subject is singular and the other subject is plural, the verb agrees with the subject closer to the verb:

    Either the students or the professor *is* wrong.
    Either the professor or the students *are* wrong.

AFFIRMATIVE AND NEGATIVE SUBJECTS

If one of two subjects is affirmative and the other negative, the verb agrees with the affirmative subject, regardless of which is nearer the verb:

The teachers, but not the principal, *were* elated to hear that the student passed the test.

Not the campus monitor but the security guards *were* stationed at the door.

ᔥ EXERCISE 4.4 ᔥ

Put a wavy line under the compound subject in each sentence; then underline the correct verb to go with it.

1. Italy and Greece (is, are) places located in the eastern Mediterranean.
2. Neither John nor his friend (accept, accepts) responsibility for the accident.
3. Gloria and her brothers (was, were) editing the term paper when the professor entered the room.
4. The carpenters and the contractors (meet, meets) every Monday to discuss the cabinetwork throughout the house.
5. Justine or Mark (has, have) visited Sweden and Denmark several times this year.
6. Hard work and determination (constitute, constitutes) financial success.
7. Bernadette or Brian (was, were) to blame for the unfortunate incident.
8. The brooms or the vacuum cleaner (was, were) left on the porch.
9. Sharon and her sisters (participate, participates) in every debate offered.
10. Either Jane or Frances (is, are) likely to be elected.

ᔥ EXERCISE 4.5 ᔥ

Put a wavy line under the subjects in the following sentences; then underline the correct verb for each subject.

1. The lightning, not the thunder, (scare, scares) me.
2. Not the students but the teachers (get, gets) on my nerves.

3. Either Mitsuko or Stella (is, are) capable of leading the group.

4. Bacon and eggs (is, are) a tasty combination.

5. Neither the children nor the parent (is, are) to blame.

6. The musician or the choir members (was, were) responsible for the failure.

7. The electrician and the plumber (work, works) well together.

8. Tenacity and courage (is, are) necessary to gain success.

9. Cooking and cleaning (is, are) not at the top of my priority list.

10. Drinking liquor and smoking cigarettes (was, were) the cause of his death.

SUBJECTS AFTER THE VERBS

The verb agrees with the subject even when the subject follows the verb, as it does in questions and after the expletives *there* and *here:* If you are unsure of the subject, ask *who* or *what* of the verb. If you are unsure of the verb, ask what the subject is doing or what the subject is having done to it.

Are there any questions?

Is Jason studying for the placement test?

♋ EXERCISE 4.6 ♋

Underline the correct verb for the subject of each sentence.

1. (Are, Is) you the culprit?

2. (Are, Is) Tony always the last one to arrive?

3. (Has, Have) he accepted the worst part of the ordeal?

VERBS WITH INDEFINITE PRONOUNS

As noted in Chapter 2, an *indefinite pronoun* does not refer to a specific person, place, or thing. Some indefinite pronouns are always singular, some are always plural, and some take either a singular or a plural verb, depending on the meaning in the sentence (review pages 23–25):

Everyone *likes* the new computer software.

But a few *like* the old software better.

All of the programmers *like* the latest version.

All *is* a mystery to the less technologically inclined.

♂ EXERCISE 4.7 ♄

Put a wavy line under the indefinite pronouns in the following sentences. Cross out the prepositional phrases. Underline the correct verbs.

1. Each of the teachers who (is, are) participating in the festival (is, are) expected to attend the meeting.
2. Everybody (know, knows) that Linus is incompetent.
3. Both (object, objects) to the final decision.
4. Everybody in close proximity to the school (was, were) looking when the bus stopped.
5. Many (offer, offers) to provide partial assistance to the two orphan boys.
6. Each of them (cause, causes) a traumatic experience whenever he is present.
7. Nobody (tell, tells) the truth anymore.
8. Several (are, is) to blame.
9. A few items (is, are) needed for the flea market on Saturday.
10. Someone (steal, steals) my gym shoes every year.

VERBS WITH COLLECTIVE NOUNS

As noted earlier, *collective nouns* may be either singular or plural, depending on whether the writer is describing the group as a unit or the individual members of the group (review pages 22–23). The verb agrees with the intended number of the collective subject:

The committee *has* reached a decision. (*Committee* is considered as one unit.)

The committee *have* decided to go their own way. (*Committee* is considered as separate individuals.)

❧ EXERCISE 4.8 ❧

*Put a wavy line under the collective nouns in the following sentences. In the blank, indicate whether each noun is acting as a unit or acting individually. Write **U** for unit and **I** for individual. Then underline the correct verbs.*

_____ 1. The faculty (has, have) decided to post their office hours on their doors.

_____ 2. The group (has, have) decided to accept the proposal.

_____ 3. The board of directors (vote, votes) themselves raises every year.

_____ 4. The committee (has, have) to accept the detailed proposal.

_____ 5. A unit of dangerous chemicals (is, are) in the chemist's flask.

_____ 6. The class (have taken, has taken) the test individually.

_____ 7. The audience (was, were) sitting quietly with their hands folded.

_____ 8. A dozen of those (was, were) shipped via express on Friday.

_____ 9. The cabinet (decide, decides) which proposals to accept.

_____ 10. A pack of dogs (eat, eats) from my trash every Tuesday.

❧ EXERCISE 4.9 ❧

Put a wavy line under each subject; then underline the verb that agrees with the subject.

1. The components of the computer (work, works) properly.

2. She (persist, persists) in swindling people out of their money.

3. If everything (go, goes) as planned, we will leave Thursday.

4. She (seem, seems) to comprehend all of the ramifications of the agreement.

5. (Are, Is) the solution to the problem clearly understood?

6. This convention (promise, promises) to be the best in the history of the association.

7. Peanut butter and jelly (is, are) healthy for children.

8. Disinfectants (was, were) in the bathroom closet.

9. I (honor, honors) my father and my mother.

10. Television and radio (is, are) forms of media.

✤ 5 ✤

Passive Voice and Consistent Verb Tense

Combining the past participle form of a verb with a form of the verb *be,* such as *am, is, was,* or *were*, results in a construction known as the *passive voice:*

Victor *was given* an award for meritorious service.

A verb is in the *active voice* when it expresses an action performed *by* its subject. A verb is in the *passive voice* when the action it expresses is performed *on* its subject. The passive voice is useful for expressing actions in which the actor is unknown or for emphasizing of the receiver of the action.

✤ EXERCISE 5.1 ✤

In the following paragraph, fill in the blanks with the passive forms of the verbs in parentheses.

Example: The play (*present*) <u>was presented</u>.

The secretary (*fire*) _____ because he stopped conceding to his supervisor's demands. He (*give*) _____ menial tasks to perform even though he was highly qualified in his field. Upon his arrival at work each morning, he (*expect*) _____ to bring coffee to his supervisor's desk. After the supervisor had his coffee each morning, the daily newspaper (*bring*) _____ to him immediately. He (*wait*) _____ on royally throughout the day. Finally, his secretary (*wear*) _____ to a frazzle and decided that enough was enough. A short while later, his co-workers (*tell*) _____ that he had resigned. The next day, the others (*give*) _____ a huge raise.

❧ EXERCISE 5.2 ❧

In the following sentences, fill in the blanks with the passive forms of the verbs in parentheses.

1. The television (*watch*) _____ 24 hours a day.
2. Mr. Yong's tenants (*give*) _____ ample time to pay their rent.
3. I (*satisfy*) _____ with my present condition.
4. The principal (*relieve*) _____ that the student surrendered to the officers.
5. The weather forecast (*deliver*) _____ by the new meteorologist.
6. Magnolia trees (*grow*) _____ on the rooftop of the 10-story building.
7. Her antique vase (*break*) _____ by her three-year-old son.
8. Candles (*light*) _____ when the electricity went off.
9. The highly intelligent people at the party (*consider*) _____ nerds.
10. I (*park*) _____ too close to the curb.

CONSISTENT VERB TENSE

Verb tenses show time differences. For example, we could write: *I felt sick yesterday. Today I feel better. Tomorrow I will feel fine.* The verbs in these sentences change tense because the writer wants to show the difference between yesterday, today, and tomorrow. Change the tense of your verbs when you want to indicate a specific change in time. Do not change needlessly from one tense to another. When writing about events in the past, use verbs in the past tense. Similarly, if action takes place in the present, use verbs in the present tense.

Incorrect: Gloria *grabbed* her lunch and *rushes* out.

Correct: Gloria *grabbed* her lunch and *rushed* out.

ᴄ EXERCISE 5.3 ᴄ

Eliminate needless changes of tense in the following paragraph. First, decide whether the paragraph should use the present or the past tense. Then change the tense of the verbs to achieve consistency. Cross out the incorrect tenses and write the correct tenses above them.

Before the alarm went off, I awake bright-eyed and bushy-tailed. Jumping hurriedly to my feet, I run to the bathroom and take a leisurely bath. After I dressed, I fix myself a big breakfast and sit down to eat. The newspaper is on the table, so I take time to read the first section before I leave for the airport. I get in my car and dashed off. Twenty minutes later, I pick up my favorite niece and bring her to my house in plenty of time for Grandmother's birthday party.

ᴄ EXERCISE 5.4 ᴄ

Eliminate the needless changes of tense in the following sentences. Cross out the incorrect tenses and write the correct tenses above them.

1. We planned our landscape and install a sprinkler system.
2. The terms of the contract were clear, so we sign it.
3. Pamela studies every night and then go to bed.
4. After I presented the paper, I walk to my room.
5. Realizing that she had no choice, she delivered the package and return home.
6. The detectives got out of the car and tells the officer to back off.
7. Their people suffered attacks by international terrorists, but they do nothing about it.
8. All of the soldiers ran into the fields and captures their rivals.
9. He drank the water and fills the glass again.
10. When the FBI came on the scene, they surrender.

PROBLEMS WITH VERBS

- Using *will* correctly

    She *thinks* she *will go.*

    This means that she *thinks* (right now) that she *will go* (at some future time).

- Using *should* and *would* correctly

    I *should* go. (This means that I *ought to* go but suggests that I do not really expect to go or want to go.)

    I *would* go. (This means that I *am willing to* go but suggests that I am not going.)

    Compound tenses with *would* sometimes suggest not willingness but past habitual action. Avoid a *would* phrase in sentences in which the simple past or the past perfect expresses your true point of view:

    Incorrect: This *would* be easier if you *would* check your entries.
    Correct: This *would* be easier if you checked your entries.

- Using *can* and *could* correctly

    Can and *could* both mean "be able to." *Can* is used to indicate the present tense, and *could* is used to indicate the past tense:

    At the present, Jennifer *can* jog 3 miles in three minutes.
    Last month, Jennifer *could* jog 2 miles in three minutes.

    Could can also be used to indicate a possibility or hope of being able to do something:

    Jennifer wishes she *could* run 5 miles in five minutes.

63

- Using *lie* and *lay* correctly

    The verb *lie* means "rest, recline, remain in a horizontal position." Its principal parts are *lie, lay, (have) lain* (present participle: *lying*). The verb *lie* never takes an object (receiver of the action).

    The verb *lay* means "put" or "place" (something). Its principal parts are *lay, laid, (have) laid* (present participle: *laying*). These forms always take an object.

Present	Past	Past Participle	Present Participle
lie ("rest")	lay	lain	lying
lay ("put")	laid	laid	laying

Lie

Occasionally, I *lie* down on the couch.

Ericka *lay* on the sand yesterday.

How long has she *lain* there?

The pencil is *lying* on the desk.

Lay

Lay the books down, please.

Peggy *laid* the papers on the desk yesterday.

Have you *laid* your papers down?

I was *laying* the books on the desk.

✌ EXERCISE 5.5 ✌

Write the correct form of the verb lie *or* lay *in the blank in each of the following sentences.*

1. The little girl was still _____ quietly in her bed.
2. Last winter, my dog often _____ in his dog house.
3. _____ down, Marie!
4. The newspaper is _____ in the rain.
5. The professor _____ his glasses on the desk and dropped his head.
6. I will _____ down and take a nap.
7. Yes, I _____ the magazine in the rack.
8. Veronica had _____ on the new mattress before.
9. The fallen trees _____ all up and down the mountain.
10. The sitter _____ the little tot down for a nap.

Complete the explanation of the correct usage of lie *and* lay *by filling in the blanks with the correct form of each verb.*

The verb (1) _____ means "put" or "place something." The present participle is (2) _____. The past and the past participle have the same form, which is (3) _____. The infinitive form is (4) _____.

The verb (5) _____ means to "rest" or "recline." The present participle is (6) _____. The past form is (7) _____, and the past participle is (8) _____.

The verb (9) _____, with all of its forms, never has an object; however, the forms of (10) _____ do have objects.

- Using *sit* and *set* correctly

  The verb *sit* means "rest in an upright, sitting position." The principal parts of *sit* are *sit, sat, (have) sat, sitting.*

  The verb *set* means "put" or "place" (something). The principal parts of *set* are *set, set, (have) set, setting.*

Present	Past	Past Participle	Present Participle
sit ("rest")	sat	sat	sitting
set ("put")	set	set	setting

Sit	*Set*
Please *sit* down.	Please *set* that down over there.
The baby *sat* on my lap.	I *set* the baby in his crib.

Remember, *sit*, like *lie*, means to be in a certain position. It never has an object. *Set*, like *lay*, means to put or place something, and it always has an object. *Set* does not change to form the past or the past participle.

Note that the verb *set* has several meanings in addition to "put" or "place":

The sun *sets*.

I *set* my watch.

You *set* a record.

John *set* out to win.

✑ EXERCISE 5.7 ✑

Write the correct form of the verb sit *or* set *in the blank in each of the following sentences.*

1. Will you _____ the flowers in the sunshine?

2. Go _____ on the courthouse steps.

3. Will Mr. Wilhelm _____ at the head of the table?

4. Energetic three-year-old children will not _____ still.

5. Those people have _____ there for three hours already.

6. Has Judy _____ in the front row all year?

7. His 1953 Chevrolet is still _____ in the garage.

8. Mother has been _____ out some flower bulbs.

9. I was _____ the cocktail table in front of the sofa when the doorbell rang.

10. On Thursday, Jonathan _____ next to Martina.

• Using *rise* and *raise* correctly

The verb *rise* means "go up." Its principal parts are *rise, rose, (have) risen, rising.* Like *lie* and *sit, rise* never takes an object.

The verb *raise* means "move (something) upward." Its principal parts are *raise, raised, (have) raised, raising.* Like *lay* and *set, raise* always takes an object.

Present	Past	Past Participle	Present Participle
rise ("go up")	rose	risen	rising
raise ("move something up")	raised	raised	raising

❧ EXERCISE 5.8 ❧

Underline the correct forms of rise *or* raise *in the following sentences.*

1. (Raise, Rise) that window as high as you can.

2. The sun (rise, rises) in the east and sets in the west.

3. I will (raise, rise) early in the morning and clean my room.

4. You (have risen, have rose) earlier than this before.

5. Park (rised, rose) from his seat when he heard the thunder.

6. Loc (rised, rose) when the ladies entered the room.

7. He (rose, raised) his hand high when they announced his name.

8. The sun was (raising, rising) as we left for the airport.

9. The peacock (rose, raised) its head and spread its tail feathers.

10. I plan to (raise, rise) your pay in approximately two months.

Review Test
Chapters 1–5

A. Circle the correct answer for each sentence.

1. The total cost of the renovation is between you and (I, me).

2. Daniel is a man (who, whom) is known for his great compassion.

3. Neither rain nor snow (is, are) in the forecast for next week.

4. The crowning of the queens (occur, occurs) every four years.

5. Seagulls (was, were) flying around the pier near the restaurant.

6. The committee (has, have) designated Friday as a casual day.

7. In (who, whom) does Drucilla trust?

8. Our Siamese cat (retrieve, retrieves) the newspaper every morning.

9. (Him and me, He and I) welcomed the newcomers to the neighborhood.

10. The mail carrier delivered the medication and (return, returned) with the payment.

11. There (is, are) several artifacts from Ancient Egypt on display at the local museum.

12. Last year our basketball team lost (its, their) final game.

13. The justice of the peace (lay, laid) the gavel on the massive, cherry desk.

14. Megan is one of those mediocre models who (need, needs) to feel important.

15. (Sit, Set) the flowers on the piano and come to me.

16. Jean's two (brother-in-laws, brothers-in-law) had difficulty reaching an amicable agreement.

17. The three (runner-ups, runners-up) trembled as they approached the gigantic stage.

18. Norman is a competent accountant who never (fail, fails) to find an error.

19. It would make sense if (you would check, you checked) your itinerary before making appointments.

20. Several clients (adhere, adheres) to the policy restrictions.

✌ 6 ✌

Verbals

Gerunds, Participles, and Infinitives

Verbals are words derived from verbs that function as nouns or other parts of speech. There are three kinds of verbals: gerunds, participles, and infinitives.

GERUNDS

A *gerund* is a verbal ending in *-ing* that is used as a noun. It is identical in form to the present participle of the verb from which it is derived (see Chapter 3). This chapter focuses on gerunds used as the subjects and objects of verbs.

Skating is dangerous. (gerund as subject)

Delivering the newspaper can become very boring. (gerund phrase as subject)

Hong loves *cooking*. (gerund as object)

Agatha loves *cooking delicious meals* for her friends. (gerund phrase as object)

✌ EXERCISE 6.1 ✌

Underline the gerund phrases used as subjects of verbs in the following sentences.

1. Reading by the fireplace is my favorite pastime.

2. Waiting for a delayed airplane to arrive infuriates me.

3. Creating new procedural manuals is time-consuming.

4. Avoiding your indebtedness by declaring bankruptcy is unfair.

5. Prosecuting innocent people causes considerable pain and suffering.

6. Articulating the organization's purpose was unnecessary.

7. Joining a Greek organization means a lot to some people.

8. Establishing credit requires patience and perseverance.

9. Dining in exclusive restaurants impresses many young women.

10. Eating a balanced diet is important to one's health.

ꙮ EXERCISE 6.2 ꙮ

Underline the gerunds or gerund phrases used as objects of verbs or complements in the following sentences.

1. Paul likes wrestling.

2. The choir members practiced harmonizing.

3. Peggy dreads driving long distances.

4. The contractor hates drilling.

5. We like watching the latest movies.

6. Fawn's most difficult decision is deciding how to respond.

7. Conchetta enjoys bathing the small doll.

8. Damon practices drawing setting-sun pictures.

9. Cindy practiced singing soprano.

10. I hate seeing you cry.

❧ EXERCISE 6.3 ❧

The following sentences contain gerunds. Complete each sentence by selecting the appropriate ending from the column at the right. Write the corresponding letter in the blank.

1. Running for office for the third time, and losing, _____.

2. Trying to reach an agreement that would satisfy everyone _____.

3. Realizing that she would not succumb to his demands, _____.

4. Scrutinizing everything that crossed her desk, _____.

5. Anticipating a huge raise, _____.

6. Declaring Angela an unfit mother, _____.

7. Assuming that we have the funds, _____.

8. Calculating the risks, _____.

9. Considering all that he has endured, _____.

10. Examining the corpse, _____.

a. Mr. Snodgrass bought a new house

b. was disheartening

c. the mortician fainted

d. she hastily threw every article in the trash

e. he perched in a corner, read a good book, and waited

f. she decided not to skip class

g. he will either become a huge success or fail drastically

h. was not easy

i. the courts awarded custody of her children to her mother

j. we will vacation in Italy or Turkey

Gerunds as Appositives

An *appositive* is a noun or pronoun that follows another noun or pronoun to identify or explain it. Like any noun or pronoun, an appositive may have adjective or adjective phrase modifiers. If it does, it is called an *appositive phrase*. Appositives are always set off with commas.

The professor's passion, *reading*, kept him up late last night. (gerund as appositive)

The professor's passion, *reading good books*, keeps him up late many nights. (gerund phrase as appositive)

❧ EXERCISE 6.4 ❧

Underline the gerunds or gerund phrases used as appositives in the following sentences. Then draw an arrow from each appositive to the word or words to which they refer.

1. Thad's talent, speaking in public, brought him great acclaim.

2. Such a misdemeanor, parking in a handicapped zone, should not be taken lightly.

3. Mr. Vinaithong's favorite task, juggling schedules, benefits the workers.

4. Delavari's best quality, volunteering to help others, motivates some people.

5. My hobby, working in the rose garden, brings me great pleasure.

PARTICIPLES

Past and present *participles* (see Chapter 3) are verb forms used as adjectives, either alone or as parts of participial phrases. Like other adjectives, they readily attach themselves to nouns and pronouns. Participles and participial phrases can also act adverbially, modifying whole clauses.

The *rising* sun cast a light across the bedroom floor. (present participle as adjective)

Defeated teams should congratulate the winners. (past participle as adjective)

Stung by his response, I could not look at him. (participial phrase as adjective)

His lecture, *interestingly enough*, was not well received. (participial phrase as sentence adverb)

❧ EXERCISE 6.5 ❧

Underline the participial phrases in the following sentences.

1. Grinning widely, Janice sauntered across the room.

2. Turning to the left, they glimpsed at the stately building.

3. The snow, coming when it did, was a welcome sight.

4. We flew to Las Vegas, having seen the points of interest in New York.

5. The professor, saddened by the student's comment, left the classroom.

6. Impressed by the dynamic report, the boss gave everyone a raise.

7. Disappointed by his girlfriend's indifference, Jeff left the party.

8. He chased the culprit through the vineyard, shouting as he ran.

9. The article, interesting to most of the participants, was discussed at length.

10. Laughing loudly, Gloria circulated the joke quickly.

INFINITIVES

An *infinitive* is the base form of a verb preceded by the word *to* (which in this particular usage is not a preposition but rather the "marker" of the infinitive). Infinitives are used as subjects, as complements, and as objects.

To laugh would be foolish. (infinitive as subject)

Her biggest goal was *to receive a doctorate degree.* (infinitive phrase as complement)

Mary hates *to clean her house.* (infinitive phrase as object)

ᕙ EXERCISE 6.6 ᕗ

*Identify the function of each of the italicized infinitives in the following sentences. Write **S** if the infinitive functions as a subject, **C** if it functions as a complement, and **O** if it functions as an object.*

_____ 1. He had hoped *to leave* at noon.

_____ 2. The person *to hire* is the person best suited for the position.

_____ 3. *To take* any other action would be inappropriate.

_____ 4. *To gain* self-confidence is a great feeling.

_____ 5. Abu's biggest mistake was *to postpone* the wedding until June.

_____ 6. Jemma loves *to play* checkers.

_____ 7. My primary objective is *to please.*

_____ 8. *To interrupt* a speaker abruptly is impolite.

_____ 9. *To articulate* well was her greatest desire.

_____ 10. *To maintain* order is the sheriff's responsibility.

✌ EXERCISE 6.7 ✌

The following sentences contain verbal phrases. Complete each sentence by selecting the appropriate ending from the column at the right. Write the corresponding letter in the blank.

1. Realizing the ramifications of not having a job, _____.
2. Dazed by the blow on the head, _____.
3. Peering at the beaming sun, _____.
4. To gain knowledge, _____.
5. Mesmerized by her beauty, _____.
6. To speak confidently, _____.
7. Hugging the curb gently, _____.
8. Disappointed with the board's vote, _____.
9. Being of sound mind and body, _____.
10. To get to the main passageway, _____.

a. he asked for a date
b. Father signed the will
c. he went to work
d. Nancy staggered
e. he left the board meeting quickly
f. you must study
g. he squinted his eyes
h. he turned the corner
i. you must be sure of yourself
j. you must turn left at the corner

✌ EXERCISE 6.8 ✌

The following sentences contain past participial forms. Complete each sentence by selecting the appropriate ending from the column at the right. Write the corresponding letter in the blank.

1. Determined to become a millionaire at any cost, _____.
2. Prepared to defend herself at any cost, _____.
3. Clouded by his personal feelings, _____.
4. Justified in firing all of them, _____.
5. Rejuvenated after her hot bath, _____.
6. Surprised by the test results, _____.
7. Angered by his son's outburst, _____.
8. Circulated all over the nation, _____.
9. Elated by her new appointment, _____.
10. Hated by the majority, _____.

a. he was biased
b. she began to make up her face
c. the paper is very well known
d. she took the day off
e. Chang did not feel guilty
f. he quickly left the room
g. Lee was not invited to the party
h. she was arrested for fraud
i. the student fainted
j. the attorney began her defense

🦢 EXERCISE 6.9 🦢

*Underline the gerund, participial, or infinitive phrases in the following sentences, and identify them in the blank. Write **G** for gerund, **P** for participle, and **I** for infinitive.*

_____ 1. Having been fishing, Marcus has smelly, clammy hands.

_____ 2. Painting a portrait is more rewarding than having one painted.

_____ 3. Playing a good game of golf is my favorite extracurricular activity.

_____ 4. To lose, as you know, is not a very good feeling.

_____ 5. Jogging the 10-mile stretch, Dr. Saini felt faint.

_____ 6. Henri, swimming the turbulent stream, was completely exhausted.

_____ 7. To acknowledge excellent work ethics is highly important.

_____ 8. Having completed your degree requirements, you should be thankful.

_____ 9. Circling the Pearson Multipurpose Center, Pat observed the robbery.

_____ 10. To learn from one's mistakes is the best way to succeed.

🦢 EXERCISE 6.10 🦢

*Underline the verbals in the following sentences and identify them in the blank. Write **G** for gerund, **P** for participle, **I** for infinitive, and **C** for complement.*

_____ 1. Being an excellent pianist, Glen Gould played with all of his heart.

_____ 2. Growing weary, she left the party before it ended.

_____ 3. Swimming in the limpid water, I observed many colorful fish.

_____ 4. To determine the cause of the fire, the arson investigators combed the area all night.

_____ 5. Cooking delectable meals is my forte.

_____ 6. Entering the contest was his claim to fame.

_____ 7. To avoid being caught, the burglar jumped from the balcony.

_____ 8. Planning the Alaskan cruise was exhilarating.

_____ 9. Feeling ill, Stephanie left the party early.

_____ 10. To travel to Europe this year might not be a good idea.

Underline the infinitives and infinitive phrases in the following selection.

To win at anything is an exhilarating feeling. But to lose is altogether different. When one wins, the pressure, struggle, and anxiety cease. The mind and body can relax, carefree at last. To understand the feeling of the losers, we must first have walked in the loser's shoes. This means that we too must have experienced loss.

Underline the gerunds and gerund phrases in the following selection.

Most people dream of acquiring economic success. However, this task requires great courage, profound dedication, and intense effort. Success is merely a dream without the focus and the insight to implement the vision. Therefore, developing a plan of action is the initial step in reaching this goal. Putting away a few dollars on a continual basis often leads to economic success. Though it might seem impossible, cutting coupons from the Sunday newspaper can also contribute to building a nest egg. Some people save thousands of dollars using this method alone. Limiting visits to restaurants that charge high prices also plays a vital role. Though elaborate foods are very tasty, they are also very expensive. Paying $40 to $50 for a small lobster is totally ridiculous for a person planning to economize. And hundreds or even thousands of dollars can be spent on tipping alone! Another good option is saving through payroll deduction. This allows a person to have money deducted before receiving his or her paycheck. Saving a designated amount of money on a weekly, biweekly, or monthly basis is an effective approach. Dreams can turn into reality by planning economic success.

7

Adjectives and Adverbs

UNDERSTANDING ADJECTIVES

Adjectives add detail to writing and make it more colorful, precise, vivid, and interesting. An adjective comes before a noun or pronoun, after a noun or pronoun, or after a linking verb.

The *bold, beautiful, multicolored* butterflies flew onto the *immaculate green-grassed* yard.

In this chapter, you will learn to identify adjectives in three ways: by their definition, by their division into classes, and by the features that distinguish them from the other parts of speech.

DEFINING ADJECTIVES

An *adjective* is a word that modifies (describes) a noun or a pronoun. Adjectives have certain characteristics that distinguish them from the noun or pronoun class. They are as follows:

- Adjectives lack plural forms.
- Adjectives can be compared.
- Adjectives themselves can be modified (described) by other words.

CLASSIFYING ADJECTIVES

- The most frequently used group of adjectives consists of *articles—a, an,* and *the:*

    A vast number of people pretend that they are happy.

    This is *an* unusual display of artwork.

    Marcus and Lin arrived at *the* auditorium at dusk.

- Proper adjectives are formed from proper nouns:

    a *British* accent

- Some adjectives describe color, shape, and manner.

    That is an unusual *green* dress.

    The *octagonal* table came from the Netherlands.

    I have an *ambivalent* feeling concerning your motives.

- Some pronouns act as adjectives in a sentence:

    They require *more.* (*More* is a pronoun.)

    We require *more* experience. (*More* is an adjective.)

The following words may be used as both pronouns and adjectives.

all	either	much	some	those
another	few	neither	such	what
any	many	one	that	which
both	more	other	these	
each	most	several	this	

- Nouns are frequently used as adjectives to describe or clarify another noun or a pronoun:

    a *peanut butter and jelly* sandwich.

- An adjective that follows a linking verb and modifies the subject is a *predicate adjective:*

    Carolyn felt *proud* after winning the card game.

IDENTIFYING ADJECTIVES BY THEIR FEATURES

Three features—degrees of comparison, intensifiers, and suffixes—may distinguish adjectives from other parts of speech.

Degrees of Comparison

- Adjectives may change forms to show differences in comparison. The three *degrees of comparison* of adjectives are *positive, comparative,* and *superlative:*

Positive degree:	I am *thin.*
Comparative degree:	You are *thinner* than I am.
Superlative degree:	Jim is the *thinnest* of the three.

    1. Use the positive degree to describe a person, place, or thing without making a comparison.
    2. Use the comparative degree to compare two persons, places, or things.
    3. Use the superlative degree to compare three or more persons, places, or things.

Positive	Comparative	Superlative
big	bigger	biggest
high	higher	highest
bad	worse	worst
good	better	best
fearful	more fearful	most fearful
promptly	more promptly	most promptly

- A modifier of one syllable usually forms its comparative and superlative by adding *-er* and *-est*, respectively.

Positive	Comparative	Superlative
soon	sooner	soonest
kind	kinder	kindest
fast	faster	fastest

- Some two-syllable modifiers form their comparative degree either by adding *-er* to the positive form or by inserting *more* before the positive form. Some two-syllable modifiers form their superlative degree either by adding *-est* to the positive form or by inserting *most* before the positive form.

- Adjectives containing three or more syllables form the comparative and superlative by adding *more* or *most* before the positive.

Positive	Comparative	Superlative
pretty	prettier	prettiest
funny	funnier	funniest
foolish	more foolish	most foolish
gracious	more gracious	most gracious

- All adjectives form negative comparisons by using *less* and *least* before the positive.

Positive	Comparative	Superlative
dangerous	less dangerous	least dangerous
articulate	less articulate	least articulate
crowded	less crowded	least crowded
junky	less junky	least junky

- A few adjectives do not follow the regular methods of forming their comparative and superlative degrees:

Positive	Comparative	Superlative
bad	worse	worst
good	better	best
much	more	most

❧ EXERCISE 7.1 ❧

Each sentence in the following paragraph contains an incorrect positive, comparative, or superlative degree. Cross out the incorrect form, and write the correct form above it. In one sentence, you need only draw a line through the incorrect form.

(1) Jennifer plays cards more better than any of her closer friends. (2) Peggy and Sue are excellent card players also, but Rachel is the worse card player in the world. (3) When she bids, she always holds the crazier hands. (4) That girl hollers more loudly than anyone in the entire room. (5) Furthermore, she slams the cards on the table with a bigger thump, grins a wider smile, and continues to play furiously. (6) One day, I was mad at her than ever before. (7) For some reason, she was playing more ridiculously than ever. (8) I jumped to my feet, stood closest to her face, and screamed in the higher-pitched voice that I could muster. (9) Sadly, she peered at me with the more innocent, big, brown eyes. (10) When the game ended, Rachel settled down and became the sweeter person on earth.

Intensifiers

- Adjectives may follow intensifiers. Intensifiers are words that modify other modifiers, including adjectives, by telling "to what extent." They include such words as *very, really, too, quite, rather*, and *fairly*.

    It was *very* difficult.

    I am *quite* sure of it.

    I am *fairly* certain that this is the solution.

    A *really* large dog sat on my hat.

Suffixes

- Most adjectives have endings that mark them as adjectives. The most common adjective suffixes are these:

Ending	Examples
-y	muddy, funny, dreamy
-ful	beautiful, faithful, sinful
-less	timeless, lawless, faithless
-en	wooden, golden, rotten
-able, -ible	likable, payable, permissible
-ive	excessive, decisive, constructive
-ous	nervous, marvelous, vigorous
-ish	selfish, mannish, boyish
-al	promotional, optional, cordial
-ic	metric, artistic, carbonic
-ary	elementary, contrary, secondary
-some	handsome, bothersome, tiresome
-ly	queenly, friendly, lonely

Be aware that these suffixes may appear on other parts of speech.

KINDS OF ADJECTIVES

- Most adjectives provide descriptive information:

  Denzel Washington is *handsome, charming,* and *talented.*
  Gothic buildings with *tall* columns are very *beautiful.*
  Cool breezes fell on the *innocent* faces of the *little* children.

- The *personal adjectives* are much like possessive pronouns. The forms are *my, our, your, his, her, its,* and *their.*

  Demetrice likes *her* hot milk before going to bed.
  Take *your* time getting to work today.

- The *definite relative adjectives* are *whose* and *which.*

  Was that the woman *whose* daughter flunked the bar examination?
  We arrived at nine, at *which* time the party was just getting started.

- The *indefinite relative adjectives* introduce noun clauses. The forms are *whose, which, what,* and their compounds with *-ever* and *-soever.*

  Whatever mistakes you make can be rectified.
  Monica decided *which* pants to wear to the reception.

  Other indefinite adjectives are *each, every, either, neither, another, any, some, both, several, all, few, enough, more, much, little, less, a, an, no other, certain,* and the cardinal (one, two, three) and ordinal numerals (first, second, third).

- The *interrogative adjectives* are used in questions. The forms are *whose, what,* and *which.*

  Whose pencil fell on the floor?
  What bus did he take?
  Which way did he travel?

- The *demonstrative adjectives* consist of *this, that, these, those,* and *such,* along with the definite article *the* and words like *latter, former, yonder, yon, very,* and *same.*

> *That* toolbox was found in the attic.
>
> The *latter* son has not lived up to their expectations.
>
> There you are, the *very* man I came to see.

೫ EXERCISE 7.2 ೪

*Underline the personal, definite relative, indefinite relative, interrogative, and demonstrative adjectives in the following sentences. In the blank, indicate the kind of adjective. Write **P** for personal, **DR** for definite relative, **IR** for indefinite relative, **I** for interrogative, and **D** for demonstrative.*

_____ **1.** That letter is deplorable!

_____ **2.** Their rented house is substandard.

_____ **3.** Igor's former chess coach was a strict disciplinarian.

_____ **4.** Which product was rejected by the Food and Drug Administration?

_____ **5.** Your transcript looks impressive.

_____ **6.** Whose beautiful handwriting is this?

_____ **7.** Several peaches were used for the peach cobbler.

_____ **8.** Is that the girl whose mother pledged a sorority at age 65?

_____ **9.** Have you ever seen such insolence?

_____ **10.** The interior decorator will decide which wallpaper to use in the model home.

Fill each blank with an appropriate and interesting adjective.

Derilyn decided to browse at the _____ antique mall adjacent to the

_____ museum. As she stepped inside the door, her _____, beautiful

eyes caught a glimpse of a _____ vase with an _____ handle on the left

side of it. It was something to behold! But as she approached the _____ aisle, she

noticed a _____ armoire. She could not believe it! "My gosh," she said, "this is

the _____ armoire that I have desperately sought for the last ten years. I must have

this _____ armoire, or I will simply die!"

͏ EXERCISE 7.4 ͏

Match the adjectives in the right column with the sentences in the left column. Place the correct letters in the spaces provided.

1. The two young men were very _____.
2. _____ grass blades waved as the wind blew furiously.
3. The _____ sports car zoomed by like a flash of lightning.
4. He asked for _____ water before he fainted.
5. Will you attend a _____ church?
6. They walked up and down the _____ trail all day long.
7. The _____ needle fell on the floor.
8. Look at the beautiful _____ floors.
9. The _____ scores were inaccurate.
10. He handed me a _____ check.

a. antique
b. Catholic
c. dusty
d. tile
e. blank
f. disposable
g. articulate
h. test
i. cold
j. Green

❧ EXERCISE 7.5 ❧

Fill each blank with an appropriate adjective to modify the noun in italics.

I dreaded getting out of bed yesterday morning because it was a _____ and _____ *day.* But I had to begin my _____ *errands.* First, I made some _____ phone *calls,* which were of top priority on my _____ *list* of things to do. Then the _____ *office* was my first errand. While there, I mailed some _____ *packages* to my publisher. I also mailed a _____ *order* to a _____ *company* in Kansas. My next stop was at the _____ *salon,* where I relaxed as my _____ *beautician* gave me a _____ *massage* before he styled my _____ *hair.* Next on my agenda were three _____ *hours* of shopping with my _____ *aunt.* We browsed in several _____ *boutiques* and a few _____ *stores* before I dropped her off at home. Finally, I pointed my _____ *car* in the direction of my _____ *job,* where I would remain for the next _____ *hours* before returning home to my _____ *husband* and my _____ *children.*

❧ EXERCISE 7.6 ❧

Revise the following sentences using appropriate, interesting adjectives to modify the nouns and pronouns. Underline the adjectives. Write the sentences on the lines provided.

1. Displaying their wings, the butterflies fluttered through the garden, landed on the roses, and flew beyond the meadow.

    _____

    _____

2. During the night in the woods, the boys heard the cry of birds and beasts.

_____

_____

3. As Angelica ate the corn, she made typewriter sounds.

_____

_____

4. The storm uprooted businesses and homes as it swept through the city.

_____

_____

5. Light blinded me as I sat on my couch in my room.

_____

_____

6. The student who cheated on the examination was severely punished.

_____

_____

7. While traveling down the road, she found a rock lying on a stump.

_____

_____

8. Tables were shipped to the office to be sold at auction.

_____

_____

9. The secretary squinted her eyes, gave me a glance, turned, and walked away.

_____

_____

10. The wind made the grass blades move in all directions.

_____

_____

Fill each blank with an appropriate and interesting adjective.

1. All _____ engineers completed their _____ tasks before they left the _____ building.

2. When we went to the zoo, we saw _____ lions, _____ kangaroos, _____ bears, and _____ snakes.

3. The _____ package toppled off the _____ shelf and hit me on my _____ head.

4. _____ particles of _____ dust covered the _____ floors of the _____ restaurant.

5. Her _____, _____ reception was the highlight of the _____ evening.

6. The aroma of the _____, _____ steaks filled the _____ room in the _____, _____ restaurant.

7. The stench of the _____, _____ medicine wafted into the _____ hospital hallways.

8. Kelsey placed her _____ eyeglasses on the _____ hot stovetop.

9. She has five _____, _____ cats and three _____ dogs.

10. The _____, _____ stallion galloped around the _____ fairgrounds.

❧ EXERCISE 7.8 ❧

Fill each pair of blanks with two interesting adjectives that describe the noun.

1. _____, _____ mold

2. _____, _____ professor

3. _____, _____ potato

4. _____, _____ computer

5. _____, _____ restaurant

6. _____, _____ lily

7. _____, _____ region

8. _____, _____ surgeon

9. _____, _____ clothing

10. _____, _____ gymnasium

✨ EXERCISE 7.9 ✨

Fill each pair of blanks with two interesting and appropriate adjectives that are close in meaning to the one already given.

1. lovely, _____, _____ girl

2. smelly, _____, _____ closet

3. good-looking, _____, _____ man

4. intelligent, _____, _____ person

5. cluttered, _____, _____ room

6. old, _____, _____ chair

7. white, _____, _____ chalk

8. large, _____, _____ building

9. checkered, _____, _____ dress

10. tattered, _____, _____ coat

UNDERSTANDING ADVERBS

Adverbs, like adjectives are words that modify. They add vivid detail to your writing, thus making it more specific and interesting. You will learn and recognize adverbs through their definition, their division into classes, and the features that distinguish them from other parts of speech.

DEFINING ADVERBS

An *adverb* is a word that modifies a verb, an adjective, or another adverb. It tells *how, how much, who, what, when, where, why, to what extent, to what degree, with what results,* or *with what concessions.* An adverb often stands next to the word it modifies but does not have to. An *-ly* ending is often a good indicator of an adverb.

When a prepositional phrase modifies a verb, an adjective, or another adverb, the phrase is an adverb phrase.

We dined *at the exclusive restaurant.*

The prepositional phrase *at the exclusive restaurant* modifies the verb *dined,* so the phrase is an adverb phrase.

CLASSIFYING ADVERBS

Most adverbs, such as *suddenly, sometimes, eagerly, quickly,* and *happily,* conform to the definition of an adverb but cannot be grouped into a special class. There are four special classes of adverbs, as follows:

- Adverbs that ask questions are called *interrogative adverbs:*

    Why don't you analyze the problem?
    Where is your sense of humor?

- A small group of adverbs is called the *affirmative and negative adverbs.* The only affirmative adverb, the word *yes,* frequently occurs as an independent element in a sentence:

    Yes, that is my decision.

    The most common negative adverbs are the words *no* and *not:*

    No, it is *not* my fault.

    The word *not* often appears as the contraction *n't* (for example, *have not* becomes *haven't*). Sometimes you must add the helping verb *do* when using the word *not:*

    Josh does *not* want a new suit.

- *Intensifiers*—adverbs that answer the question *to what extent?*—can modify both adjectives and adverbs. Intensifiers always come directly in front of the words they modify. Some common intensifiers are *very, too, completely, quite, rather, somewhat, unusually, extremely, totally,* and *so.* Adverbs modify verbs by answering the question *how?*

    All of the participants moved *slowly* toward the platform. (adverb modifying verb)
    Courtney is a *very* beautiful girl. (adverb modifying adjective)
    She performed *tremendously* well in practice last week. (adverb modifying adverb)

- Sometimes *nouns*—especially those naming a time or a place—can be used as adverbs.

IDENTIFYING ADVERBS BY THEIR FEATURES

Two features, degrees of suffixes and comparison, help to differentiate adverbs from other parts of speech.

Suffixes

- Most adverbs end in *ly:*

quietly	nervously	fearfully	enthusiastically
silently	skillfully	smoothly	aggressively

- Other adverbs do not end in *ly:*

never	often	seldom
now	then	very

Degrees of Comparison

- Like adjectives, adverbs change forms to show differences in comparison. The three *degrees of comparison* of adverbs are *positive, comparative,* and *superlative:*

Positive degree: I talk *fast.*
Comparative degree: I talk *faster* in the evening than in the morning.
Superlative degree: I talk *fastest* when I'm on the phone.

1. Use the positive degree when not making a comparison.
2. Use the comparative degree when comparing two events or circumstances.
3. Use the superlative degree when comparing three or more events or circumstances.

- Many short adverbs form the comparative and superlative degrees by adding *-er* and *-est,* respectively.

Positive	Comparative	Superlative
soon	sooner	soonest
slow	slower	slowest

- Other adverbs use *more* or *less* to form the comparative and *most* or *least* to form the superlative.

Positive	Comparative	Superlative
happily	more happily	most happily
rapidly	less rapidly	least rapidly

- A few adverbs do not follow the regular methods for forming the comparative and the superlative.

Positive	Comparative	Superlative
much	more	most
little	less	least
well	better	best
badly	worse	worst

☙ EXERCISE 7.10 ❧

Put a wavy line under the adverbs, and underline the words they modify. Remember that adverbs do not have to stand next to the words they modify. Some sentences contain adverb phrases.

1. I saw many beautiful architectural buildings as I drove speedily down the freeway.
2. She died as she had lived, peacefully.
3. According to her best friend, her mouth runs 100 miles a minute.
4. Patricia's eyeglasses lay there next to the piano.
5. We looked with amazement as the model glided gracefully to the stage.
6. Hortense cut the meat awkwardly.
7. Gene Kelley danced marvelously in all his movies.
8. She ran awkwardly across the street.
9. They were graciously greeted when they entered the room.
10. He plays because the coach is his father.

❧ EXERCISE 7.11 ❧

Put a wavy line under the adverbs, and underline the words they modify. Some sentences contain adverb phrases.

1. I stood next to the Golden Gate Bridge in San Francisco and had my picture taken.
2. The mountain climber breathed deeply as we helped him take his last step.
3. Many of the students were disturbed because they did not pass the test.
4. She dieted to lose weight.
5. Amanda was selected because she was more qualified than the other contestants.
6. The little dog moaned loudly while waiting for the vet to arrive.
7. Mark danced gracefully around the ballroom floor.
8. We marched skillfully around the courthouse in protest of the new law.
9. Joquan jumped excitedly when his name was called.
10. The horse pranced awkwardly around the barn.

❧ EXERCISE 7.12 ❧

Put a wavy line under the adverbs, and underline the words they modify.

1. Please provide a very good excuse for your absenteeism.
2. This antique car is painfully difficult to maneuver.
3. Thomas the Great remains a totally spellbinding magician in the Los Angeles area.
4. A Mercedes sedan is too conservative for Damon's flamboyant lifestyle.
5. Sunsets are amazingly beautiful this time of the year.
6. Extraordinarily knowledgeable experts were at the scene of the accident.
7. The extremely talented flutist played at her reception.
8. Your honesty is very important for the success of our relationship.
9. The upscale office contained exquisitely carved Oriental tables.
10. The extremely thorough researcher presented his in-depth report.

❧ EXERCISE 7.13 ❧

Put a wavy line under the adverbs, and underline the adverbs they modify. Some sentences contain adverb phrases.

1. Brian played the keyboard exceedingly well at the banquet last night.
2. Some people make small things unnecessarily difficult.
3. The waves moved very rapidly toward the shoreline.
4. You will feel very well once you have taken a nap.
5. Each question was so deeply embarrassing.
6. Hortense moves too slowly to win the prize.
7. Answering the question was so painstakingly difficult.
8. Words come to me very quickly.
9. I will come to see you really soon.
10. She handled the unfortunate situation tremendously well.

❧ EXERCISE 7.14 ❧

*Indicate in the blanks whether the italicized words in the following sentences are adjectives or adverbs. Write **Adj** for adjective and **Adv** for adverb.*

_____ 1. The *disgusted* delegates left the convention in an uproar.

_____ 2. *Quaint* antique shops were at every intersection.

_____ 3. She moved *aimlessly* toward the center of the room.

_____ 4. The *moldy* bread lay on his desk for three days and smelled

_____   *awful* when we opened the package.

_____ 5. Jennifer crossed Main Avenue, *reluctantly*.

_____ 6. While driving *speedily* down the highway, he struck an

_____   *oncoming* car.

_____ 7. *Notorious* outlaws stopped and ate at the Stagecoach Inn in Salado, Texas.

_____ 8. The new department store will open *soon*.

_____ 9. Grace Jones is an *upscale* boutique where movie stars shop.

_____ 10. Yuka stood patiently by the *front* door and didn't say a word.

❧ EXERCISE 7.15 ❧

Write 9 sentences using adverbs effectively. Write three sentences containing adverbs modifying adjectives, three sentences containing adverbs modifying verbs, and three sentences containing adverbs modifying adverbs.

1. _____

   _____ .

2. _____

   _____ .

3. _____

   _____ .

4. _____

   _____ .

5. _____

   _____ .

6. _____

   _____ .

7. _____

   _____ .

8. _____

   _____ .

9. _____

   _____ .

Underline the correct adjectives and adverbs in the following sentences.

(1) Brian and Jessica always sneak (quiet, quietly) into the classroom. (2) However, Brian walks more (quick, quickly) than Jessica does. (3) As a result, the teacher never sees him, and she thinks that he is a (really, real) punctual guy. (4) But Jessica gains favor with the teacher also; she works (good, well) with all of her classmates. (5) Since Brian is not as smart as Jessica, being late will probably cause him to earn (poorly, poor) grades.

AVOIDING DOUBLE NEGATIVES

When two negative words are used where only one is necessary, the construction is called a *double negative*. Double negatives should be avoided in most written contexts.

Incorrect: I did*n't* do *nothing* wrong. (Both *n't* and *nothing* are negative.)
Correct: I did*n't* do anything wrong.
Correct: I did *nothing* wrong.

Do not use *not* with *hardly, scarcely, no, nothing,* and *none* when making a negative statement:

Incorrect: I do*n't hardly* ever see a good movie.
Correct: I *hardly* ever see a good movie.

Do not use *not* when using the words *only* and *but* to mean "no more than":

Incorrect: I do*n't* have *but* two dresses.
Correct: I have *but* two dresses.

Underline all the adjectives in the following selection.

As Aunt Jennifer and I drove into the huge parking lot, we gazed upon a neat, stately, brick building surrounded by green grass and lots of mature trees. "This is a very nice place," I said with some astonishment. "Look at the beautiful lawn." Then we saw her—my dear Aunt Pearl, Jennifer's older sister—walking up the massive concrete stairway, having a fascinating conversation with herself. Her frail body was stooped from age. Aunt Jennifer and I walked slowly behind her, observing her every move. After she closed the door to her room, we knocked. The door opened to reveal a gray-haired, elderly lady who was so surprised to see us, she let out a little gasp. I said, "Hi, Aunt Pearl—this is a really nice place. It's great that you can sit on the bed and look out the window at the green grass and trees. Why, you can even see the cars as they pass by." Aunt Pearl peered at me with the strangest expression on her lined face. "Would *you* want to live here?" she asked. That question caught me off guard. I gave her a wry smile and changed the subject.

I spoke quietly to Aunt Jennifer about matters concerning her feisty older sister, who, I thought, surely wasn't aware of our conversation. But to my surprise, Aunt Pearl interrupted us, saying, "I could hear every word you said, and I saw you wink your shifty little eye. I'm not deaf, you know." I answered with a warm smile. "Aunt Pearl, I'm sorry; I thought you were busy with your own things." She brightened and said, "Would you all like some chocolate chip cookies?" As she looked for the cookies, she said, "That old man ate all of my cookies. They were good, too." She opened her nightstand drawer, and there lay one lone cookie and a half-eaten bologna sandwich. She exclaimed, "Oh, I didn't know that was there."

Pearl removed a new pair of navy blue shoes from her closet and gave them to Jennifer, who wore the same size as she did. She searched through all of her dresser drawers. She then removed large quantities of clothes from her closet and went on and on about how nice they were and how she liked to look nice. You see, every day she dresses as if she were going out to an elaborate place for the evening. We commented on how beautiful her clothes were. I could tell by the expression on her face that she was very proud of her possessions and that she was so happy that we liked them. As the day wore on, she spoke about many subjects. We sat and listened, commenting every now and then.

At the end of our visit, we all walked down the massive stairway. As we reached the bottom step, we ran into one of Aunt Pearl's new neighbors. She said to her friend, "Hello, Amanda. That lady is my sister," pointing toward my aunt. Then, taking my hand, she said, "I'm not sure who this young lady is, but she is certainly very nice."

◌ EXERCISE 7.18 ◌

Underline all the adverbs in the following selection.

It was one of those days, destined to go wrong—destined to be challenging. I awakened to the sound of birds merrily chirping and the sun shining brightly on my face. I couldn't believe it! It was 8:50 in the morning. I scurried hurriedly into the bathroom, and in nothing flat I had taken care of all the necessary things pertaining to my personal hygiene. There was no time to delight in that usual cup of coffee or that bowl of wheat cereal that I had become accustomed to each morning. In 20 minutes, I was frantically running out the back door, making my way to the car. It was one of the fastest drives in history!

I arrived at the school at 9:30 on the dot. As I approached the door, I noticed that there weren't any students inside the classroom. There was a note hanging loosely on the door. It read, "Do not enter. Virus inside!" I looked up the hallway, and there they were, the entire second-grade class. One student moved hurriedly toward me, screaming, "Mrs. Henry, don't go into the classroom. There is a virus in there!" I dropped my briefcase in the hallway and laughed hysterically until I cried. You see, the virus to which they alluded was a computer virus. I am totally convinced that it would have been far better if computer glitches could have been diagnosed as having anything except medical problems. Later, I explained to the students that computers become infected with "viruses" that cause them to malfunction. I further informed them that these viruses occur for many reasons, such as unclean disks or exposure to unsafe weather conditions, and that sometimes the computer programmers set the computers to malfunction on a particular day just for the heck of it. That virus ruined what would have been a very productive class period. But we just couldn't concentrate on the matter of academics, for we were too busy laughing and talking constantly about that great illness. Even now, when I think about that day, I burst out laughing—either aloud or in the privacy of my soul. It was just one of those crazy days.

8

Prepositions

UNDERSTANDING PREPOSITIONS

Prepositions help words work together in sentences by showing relationships among words. Learning the definition of prepositions and recognizing their role in a sentence are two ways of studying this part of speech.

DEFINING PREPOSITIONS

Prepositions function as connectives. They connect nouns or pronouns to some other part of the sentence and show the relationship involved. Prepositions indicate such relations as direction, position, and duration.

Simple Prepositions

aboard	alongside	behind	but (meaning "except")	for
about	amid	below	by	from
above	among	beneath	concerning	in
across	around	beside	despite	inside
after	as	besides	down	into
against	at	between	during	like
along	before	beyond	except	near

Simple Prepositions

nearer	onto	round	toward	upon
nearest	out	since	under	with
next	outside	through	underneath	within
of	over	throughout	until	without
off	past	till	unto	
on	regarding	to	up	

Compound Prepositions

according to	due to	in spite of
along with	except for	instead of
apart from	from across	next to
aside from	from among	on account of
as for	from between	out of
as regards	from under	owing to
as to	in addition to	prior to
as well as	in case of	up to
because of	in front of	with reference to
by means of	in lieu of	with regard to
by reason of	in place of	with respect to
by way of	in regard to	with the exception of

RECOGNIZING PREPOSITIONAL PHRASES

A *prepositional phrase* consists of the preposition, its object, and any modifiers the object may have:

The clothes *in the closet* have been cleaned. (*In* is the preposition, *the* is the modifier, and *closet* is the object.)

In most cases, the preposition follows immediately after the word that is modified by the prepositional phrase. However, occasionally the prepositional phrase is put at the beginning of the clause. In that case, the prepositional phrase should be followed by a comma:

With a very sharp needle, the doctor pricked the patient's finger.

If a verb follows the prepositional phrase, no comma should be used:

Through the door walked a stunning model.

❧ EXERCISE 8.1 ❧

Underline all the prepositional phrases in the following sentences.

1. That comment put me in a precarious situation.
2. The nursery rhyme stated that the cow jumped over the moon.
3. She ran around the corner and caught the bus.
4. Due to extenuating circumstances, the case was dismissed.
5. The little excursion sent us down the street, around the corner, and into the courtyard.
6. Their mother divided the candy among them.
7. Always cut your meat across the grain, not with it.
8. During the winter months, I use my fireplace a great deal of the time.
9. Work in the flowerbed nearest the house.
10. We will stay at home on account of the weather.

EXERCISE 8.2

Select the appropriate prepositional phrase to complete each sentence. Write the corresponding letter in the blank.

1. The beautiful stallion pranced _____.
2. Her credentials were placed _____.
3. What is the price of 3 pounds _____?
4. The prisoners escaped _____.
5. Katrina will receive $3,000 _____.
6. Veronica's mother found the pots and pans _____.
7. Administer the medicine _____.
8. We chose Sonia _____.
9. Gloria found her favorite socks _____.
10. Of the stars near the earth, Sirius _____.

a. besides her $1,000 bonus
b. according to the directions
c. into the barn
d. on her office wall
e. underneath the cabinet
f. of fresh lobster
g. as secretary
h. from bondage
i. is the brightest
j. between the sheets

EXERCISE 8.3

Supply appropriate prepositions to complete the following statements.

1. I have learned a lot _____ astronomy.
2. The ears _____ rabbits are long and floppy.
3. A fish cannot stay out _____ the water for very long.
4. We have been the best of friends _____ the years.
5. Statistics reveal that most thefts occur _____ the day.
6. I always drink two cups of coffee _____ the morning.
7. A horse is considered old _____ the age _____ thirty.
8. Equipped _____ a type _____ radar, a bat squeaks _____ a high pitch.
9. We drove _____ Virginia Beach last year.
10. Davion moved _____ the edge _____ the pool.

Write 10 sentences in which you use prepositional phrases effectively. Use as many different prepositions as possible.

1. _____
   _____

2. _____
   _____

3. _____
   _____

4. _____
   _____

5. _____
   _____

6. _____
   _____

7. _____
   _____

8. _____
   _____

9. _____
   _____

10. _____
    _____

EXERCISE 8.5

In the following sentences, underline each preposition. Then draw an arrow from the preposition to its object.

1. During the morning, he delivers newspapers.
2. He always had several women after him.
3. The girl with the big, blue eyes was fascinated by his romantic glances.
4. Otis toiled up the mountain and found his binoculars.
5. The author studied many books on Europe before writing his book about European lifestyles.
6. Laughing like an idiot, James ran to the center of the room and fell on the floor and kicked.
7. Pauline wore a huge ring on her finger and a beautiful bracelet on her wrist.
8. As I sat in the barber's chair, I thought about the good old times.
9. She returned from the store in a few minutes and prepared the meal.
10. We waited until dark to begin the fireworks.

EXERCISE 8.6

Underline the prepositional phrases in the following sentences. Put an additional wavy line under the preposition in each phrase.

1. I breathed a sigh of relief when he walked into the room.
2. He looked beyond my faults and saw my need.
3. The candle fell off the table during the night and burned the dresser.
4. Tomeka looked down the street and saw the ambulance coming.
5. The computer analyst searched the Internet throughout the night.
6. The doctor measured the circumference of the baby's head.
7. They ate popcorn and candy during the intermission and went to dinner after the movie.
8. There are many sunny beaches in Florida.
9. Andrew was told that he was within his rights.
10. What do you like to do besides read all day?

ᘒ EXERCISE 8.7 ᘒ

Underline all the prepositional phrases in the following selection. Put an additional wavy line under the preposition in each phrase.

The Systems of the Human Body

The *skeletal system* is composed of bones and the cartilaginous and membranous structures associated with them. This system protects and supports the soft parts of the body and supplies levers for body movement. Connective tissue predominates in this area.

The *muscular system* is composed of muscles, fasciae, tendon sheaths, and bursae. The three types of muscles are striated, moving the skeleton; smooth, found along the alimentary tract; and cardiac, found in the heart.

The *nervous system* consists of the brain, the spinal cord, cranial nerves, peripheral nerves, and sensory and motor terminals. It is the correlating and controlling system of the body, intimately connected with the other systems and with the outside world. Special senses include vision, hearing, taste, and smell.

The *circulatory system* comprises the heart, veins, lymph vessels, arteries, and capillaries. It pumps and distributes the blood carrying oxygen, nutrients, and wastes.

The *respiratory system* is composed of the air sinuses, larynx, pharynx, trachea, bronchi, and lungs. It is involved in bringing oxygen to the blood and in eliminating carbon dioxide from the blood.

The *digestive system* includes the alimentary tract, with the associated glands, from the lips to the anus. It converts food into simpler substances that can be absorbed and used by the body.

The *urinary system* comprises the kidneys, ureters, urinary bladder, and urethra. Its chief functions are the formation and elimination of urine and the maintenance of homeostasis.

The *endocrine system* includes the hypophysis (pituitary), thyroid, parathyroids, suprarenals, pancreatic islets in the pancreas, ovaries, testes, pineal body, and placenta (during pregnancy). The endocrine glands are involved in the chemical regulation of body functions.

The *reproductive system* consists of the ovaries, uterine tubes, uterus, vagina, and vulva in the female and the testes, seminal vesicles, penis, prostate, and urethra in the male. It functions in the perpetuation of the species.

~ 9 ~

Conjunctions

UNDERSTANDING CONJUNCTIONS

Like prepositions, conjunctions show the relationship between words or groups of words in a sentence. You can identify conjunctions by learning their definition and the classes into which they can be grouped.

DEFINING CONJUNCTIONS

A *conjunction* is a word whose primary function is to join words or groups of words.

CLASSIFYING CONJUNCTIONS

The two main types of conjunctions are *coordinating* and *subordinating* conjunctions.

COORDINATING CONJUNCTIONS

The coordinating conjunctions are *and, but, for, nor, or, so,* and *yet*. (*For* is a conjunction when it means "because"; otherwise, it is a preposition.)

Coordinating conjunctions are used to connect sentence elements of the same grammatical class—for instance, nouns with nouns, adverbs with adverbs, phrases with phrases, and clauses with clauses.

- The conjunctions *and, but,* and *or* may be used to connect any sentence elements of the same class:

Joining nouns:	<u>Ben Woods</u> *and* <u>LaShawn Cohen</u> are very good friends.
Joining verbs:	The preacher <u>got up</u> *and* <u>walked away</u>.
Joining adjectives:	The professor is <u>intelligent</u> *but* <u>lazy</u>.
Joining prepositional phrases:	The cow had to <u>cross the river</u> *or* go <u>into the meadow</u>.

- *For, yet*, and *so* are used to connect main clauses:

  I knew spring was coming, *for* the birds were chirping outside my window.
  She loves him very much, *yet* she doubts his love for her.
  George did not trust Angela, *so* he called her on the telephone every 30 minutes.

- Note that a comma must be placed before the conjunction when a conjunction is used to connect two complete sentences (main clauses).

- *Yet* may also be used as a conjunction in a compound subject or predicate:

  It's a simple *yet* amusing little wine.
  That's an odd observation *yet* quite accurate.

❧ EXERCISE 9.1 ❧

Underline the appropriate coordinating conjunction for each sentence.

1. Courtney (for, and) Shervett are sisters.
2. Swimming (yet, and) bowling classes are held at the gymnasium.
3. Delores is neither pretty (for, nor) ugly.
4. We will either pay the price (for, or) stay at home.
5. They will never accept her resignation, (but, for) she is a diligent worker.
6. You can carry my bag (nor, or) pay the hotel bill.
7. I cannot believe that she made that statement, (yet, for) she is usually a compassionate individual.
8. Rosita has a nasty attitude, (or, but) she gets the job done.
9. I will not forgive you, (or, nor) will I recommend you for the position.
10. I got a good night's sleep, (for, yet) I feel exhausted.

❧ EXERCISE 9.2 ❧

Underline the coordinating conjunctions in the following sentences.

1. Archibald is smart but unreliable.
2. Dimitri loves ice skating, yet he hates cold weather.
3. Nancy has never been to Switzerland, nor has she been to Norway.
4. There were complications with her pregnancy, but the baby was healthy.
5. You will be honored Saturday night, for you have done exemplary community service.
6. We received the "Yard of the Month" recognition, for we had a beautiful yard.
7. Either Constance will tell the truth, or she will lose the respect of her friends.
8. My supervisor treats me badly, yet I do not shirk my responsibilities.
9. She does not have a master's degree, but she does have a bachelor's degree.
10. Tenacity and self-confidence are important personal attributes.

✢ EXERCISE 9.3 ✢

Examine the italicized coordinating conjunctions in the following sentences. If a conjunction is used correctly, write OK above it. If it is used incorrectly, cross it out and write a correct conjunction above it.

1. The children played cheerfully, *yet* they had a lot of fun.
2. The computer had a virus, *nor* we used it anyway.
3. My calculation is correct, *for* you will pay the bill.
4. He is a dedicated volunteer, *yet* we plan to honor him Friday night.
5. Playing the piano is difficult, *or* I practiced into the night.
6. I have studied for the exam for 13 hours, *yet* I am not weary.
7. Henri is not the best speller in the class, *but* he is the best writer.
8. Our college closed the cafeteria, *yet* the food was horrible.
9. The workshop proved informative, *for* the speaker was boring.
10. Reading, writing, *and* golfing are excellent hobbies.

✢ EXERCISE 9.4 ✢

In the following sentences, circle each coordinating conjunction and underline the words, phrases, or clauses that they join.

1. Parallel parking was easy, but backing up was difficult.
2. Good sense and sound advice have helped me tremendously.
3. My aunt Esther is witty and wise.
4. The burglar went around the corner and broke into the library.
5. Either Charles or Otis will become chairman when Andrew relinquishes his position.
6. A hefty bonus or a raise will suffice.
7. In the meantime, you will either apply for the position or enroll in college full time.
8. Either the airplanes are late or the flight attendants are rude.
9. Learning to play dominoes and learning to play cards were easy.
10. The diamond was brilliant, but it was small.

❧ EXERCISE 9.5 ❧

Underline all the coordinating conjunctions in the following sentences.

1. Henrietta, but not Jennifer, danced.
2. Writing novels and writing textbooks are completely different.
3. I have experienced many bad days in my life, but my good days outweigh my bad days.
4. This task is not easy, yet I will stick to it until the end.
5. My granddaughter wants everything, for she has not learned the value of a dollar.
6. The dress was too small, but I bought it anyway.
7. Things got out of control, but the officer intervened and returned things to normal.
8. I am neither happy nor sad concerning the situation.
9. Justice should prevail, yet it doesn't always.
10. There was nothing we could do, for we were too far gone.

❧ EXERCISE 9.6 ❧

Supply an appropriate coordinating conjunction for each sentence.

1. Neither rain _____ snow will hinder me from driving my new car today.
2. The stakes are high, _____ I will take my chances.
3. Either Damon _____ Manuel will tackle the difficult plumbing job.
4. The barber _____ the beautician entered the competition.
5. Technicians repaired the computer glitch, _____ the engineers completed their tasks after all.
6. John did not have any money in the bank, _____ he wrote a check anyway.
7. She accepted his marriage proposal, _____ a good man is hard to find.
8. Lorna was very disappointed, _____ no one knew why.
9. We all face choices in life, _____ many times we make the wrong ones.
10. I searched everywhere, _____ she was not to be found.

Complete each sentence by adding a coordinating conjunction and other words necessary to make a complete sentence. Add punctuation where necessary.

   1. Circumstances have changed _____

   _____

   2. You were adamant concerning the postponement of the proposal, _____

   _____

   3. Mr. Markson looks highly distinguished, _____

   _____

   4. These are considered extenuating circumstances, _____

   _____

   5. The diagnosticians were confident, _____

   _____

   6. She was once very adept at calligraphy, _____

   _____

   7. Detailed information was provided _____

   _____

   8. The detective continued to search for the stolen jewelry _____

   _____

   9. All of the young attorneys passed the examination, _____

   _____

  10. Sparrows flitted around my back door _____

   _____

❧ EXERCISE 9.8 ❧

Supply an appropriate coordinating conjunction in each of the following sentences.

   1. The flutist left for the wedding, _____ he left his flute at home.

   2. This filing system is antiquated, _____ it has not been updated since 1938.

   3. It has not rained in two months, _____ this will not be a good year for farmers.

4. The Constitution states that all people are equal under the law, _____ racial biases still exist.

5. Jeffrey received his new title in February, _____ it will not be reflected on his paycheck until June.

6. I found the book entertaining, _____ it lacked substance.

7. Some jobs are personally rewarding _____ financially insecure.

8. Swimming _____ running are two major weight-losing exercises.

9. Jermiah works constantly, _____ he never has any money.

10. Strangely enough, the sun was beaming on my face, _____ the wind was cutting my back.

✂ EXERCISE 9.9 ✂

Write 10 sentences using coordinating conjunctions. Demonstrate coordinating conjunctions joining nouns with nouns, verbs with verbs, adjectives with adjectives, phrases with phrases, and clauses with clauses.

1. _____

_____

2. _____

_____

3. _____

_____

4. _____

_____

5. _____

_____

6. _____

_____

7. _____

_____

8. _____

_____

9. _____

_____

10. _____

_____

SUBORDINATING CONJUNCTIONS

Subordinating conjunctions connect subordinate clauses to main clauses and show the relation between them. Such conjunctions often introduce adverb clauses. The most commonly used subordinating conjunctions are *when, whenever, where, wherever, because, unless, until, till, though, although, even though, as though, while, before, after, as, if, as if, as long as, as soon as, whether, so that, provided, provided that, except that, in order that, whereas, than,* and *since.*

Subordinate means "lesser in rank or importance." Whenever a clause starts with one of the listed conjunctions, you know that there has to be at least one more clause in the sentence and that at least one of the other clauses must be an independent clause. Subordinate clauses need independent clauses to complete their meaning.

Subordinate clauses may be placed either before or after the core sentence (complete thought). When you place the subordinate clause before the core sentence, you must use a comma after the clause to indicate where the subordinate clause ends and the core sentence begins. When the subordinate clause is placed after the core sentence, a comma is usually not used.

Dew, *which is moisture condensed from the atmosphere,* was on my grass this morning. (adjective clause)

In this sentence, the subordinate adjective clause, *which is moisture condensed from the atmosphere,* is subordinate to the rest of the sentence. Notice that the subordinate clause is in the middle of the sentence.

If time permits, we will watch a second movie. (adverb clause)

116

In this sentence, the subordinate clause is placed at the beginning of the sentence; therefore, you know that the independent clause must follow the punctuation.

Dinner was ready *before the guests arrived.* (adverb clause)

In this sentence, the subordinate clause follows the independent, with no intervening punctuation.

Noun clauses are usually introduced by *that, what, whatever, who, whoever, whom,* or *whomever:*

Jeremy thought *that I knew.* (noun clause)
We could tell *who he was.* (noun clause)

➳ EXERCISE 9.10 ❧

Select the appropriate subordinating conjunction for each sentence. Write the letter for the correct answer in the blank.

1. _____ you pay all of the expenses, we will take a trip.	**a.** Before
2. _____ the itinerary was planned, the executive left for the airport.	**b.** If
	c. Though
3. _____ I see you, I will give you a big hug.	**d.** Because
4. _____ you plan to attend the conference, please take notes for me.	**e.** As
	f. When
5. _____ she does not like you, she will insult your intelligence.	**g.** Provided that
6. _____ Meg values her mother's opinion, she relies on her own instinct.	**h.** Since
	i. After
7. _____ this is the only opportunity I have, I think I will take it.	**j.** Whereas
8. _____ you leave home, do not forget to turn the stove off.	
9. _____ you are sitting in the beautician's chair, you might as well study.	
10. _____ you study diligently, you will become successful in life.	

Select an appropriate subordinating conjunction for each sentence from the following options: until, although, that, unless, as if, if, before, since, so that, while, whether, whenever, *and* which. *Do not use any conjunction more than once.*

1. _____ I hear from you in the next 20 minutes, I am leaving.

2. _____ you entertain the idea, we are no longer friends.

3. Connie is saving her money _____ she can purchase a home in the new development.

4. _____ I am not altogether against your plan, I am also not for it.

5. James enrolled in English 122 _____ he was not prepared for English 233.

6. _____ the circumstantial evidence is very strong, I doubt that there will be a conviction.

7. This is the dress _____ Betty wore to the dance.

8. Do not turn the page _____ I tell you to turn it.

9. It looks _____ if a hailstorm might come.

10. _____ you go or not, I will.

Combine the columns to make complete sentences. In each blank, write the letter of the clause that will complete the sentence. Add punctuation where necessary.

1. Melody came _____.

2. Jennifer passed the test _____.

3. If I catch you cheating _____.

4. Because you are pretty _____.

5. Unless you stop procrastinating _____.

a. you attract all the good-looking guys.

b. he will faint.

c. we might arrive on time.

d. whereas Lois flunked it.

e. although she was not invited.

6. Since I know nothing about computers _____.

7. After she clears all of her debt _____.

8. We left early in order that _____.

9. Justin looks as if _____.

10. After a wet spell _____.

f. insects come out of hiding.

g. I will cut your paper in two.

h. you will never complete the project.

i. I will take a computer basics course.

j. she plans to buy a new car.

ᔓ EXERCISE 9.13 ᖇ

Supply appropriate subordinating conjunctions for the following sentences, adding punctuation where necessary. Do not use any conjunction more than once. When you are satisfied with your responses, exchange papers with a classmate and compare answers.

1. All of the circumstantial evidence incriminated him _____ he was found guilty beyond a shadow of a doubt.

2. She quickly jumped out of the car _____ her stomach was upset.

3. _____ the first two chapters are indicative of good work, then the rest of the chapters must be good also.

4. He borrowed my card table and chairs _____ he was having a party.

5. _____ the radio played, we danced to the oldies tunes.

6. _____ Monica started dating, she did not realize that staying out late could be dangerous.

7. Antonio will help you with your accounting _____ you will help him with his French.

8. The man decided to work really hard _____ he could open a fast-food restaurant.

9. _____ I have a conscience, I cannot betray my friends.

10. He had a way of making people happy _____ he was penniless.

The following sentences are written with the subordinate clauses before the core sentences. The ideas are confusing because there is no indication where the subordinate clauses end. Correct the sentences by supplying the appropriate punctuation.

1. Whenever Jean and Frances visit other countries they buy souvenirs for everyone.
2. If the car you bought has a CD player you may have some of my CDs.
3. When they installed a ceiling fan on their patio the breeze it created cooled everyone instantly.
4. Because the oak tree was so old and wobbly Tarrence had to cut it down.
5. Since my sister invited me to dinner I did not have to cook Sunday.
6. Until I started exercising I weighed 160 pounds.
7. Although it's springtime the weather is still a little cool.
8. Before you draw inferences please have all the facts.
9. Unless you plan to move soon you need to remodel your kitchen.
10. Because he was not a good repairman we had to pay someone else to do the job.

🔊 **EXERCISE 9.15** 🔊

*In each of the following sentences, underline the subordinate clause, and add punctuation where necessary. In the blank, identify each clause as an adjective (**Adj**), adverb (**Adv**), or noun (**N**) clause.*

_____ 1. When I took my granddaughter to Sea World last summer she had a great time.
_____ 2. Tell me whom you saw.
_____ 3. Here is the book for which I have been searching.
_____ 4. This is the gown that I want.
_____ 5. After the discovery of the lost gem was made known people stopped looking for it.
_____ 6. In the closet are the tennis shoes that Veronica wore.
_____ 7. I will get even with you if it takes a lifetime.
_____ 8. If you take my advice you will not be sorry.
_____ 9. Your instructions were easy to follow because they were clear and simple.
_____ 10. Though you left early you didn't miss a thing.

❧ EXERCISE 9.16 ❧

Write 10 sentences using subordinating conjunctions. Place some conjunctions at the beginning of the sentences and some conjunctions in the middle of the sentences. Do not use any conjunction more than once.

1. _____

_____

2. _____

_____

3. _____

_____

4. _____

_____

5. _____

_____

6. _____

_____

7. _____

_____

8. _____

_____

9. _____

_____

10. _____

_____

EXERCISE 9.17

Make the following sentences complete by adding independent clauses to them. Place some of the subordinate clauses at the beginning of the sentences and some in the middle of the sentences. Add punctuation and capitalization where they are needed.

1. because he had a desire to sing

   _____

   _____

2. before you judge me

   _____

   _____

3. since Darcus filed for a divorce

   _____

   _____

4. as you reflect on the past five years

   _____

   _____

5. as if the whole world has turned against him

   _____

   _____

6. while the band played soft music

   _____

   _____

7. although you procrastinated

   _____

   _____

8. when the newspaper article appeared on the front page

   _____

   _____

9. until things change drastically

   _____

   _____

10. after a lengthy wait in the registration line

    _____

    _____

CONJUNCTIVE ADVERBS

Conjunctive adverbs are transitional words that are at least partly adverbial, although they connect two independent clauses and modify the second. Some commonly used conjunctive adverbs are *nevertheless, however, moreover, hence, consequently, nonetheless, accordingly, then, besides, likewise, indeed,* and *therefore.* Unlike the other connectives, they may stand at many points in the given sentence.

Some other conjunctive adverbs are *in the meantime, on the other hand, that is, in the first place,* and *on that account.*

All of the bridges were closed; *consequently,* we could not get to work on time.

Alice was sad because she had lost her ticket to the performance; she seems, *however,* to be recovering from her disappointment.

Pearline did not agree with her boss's tactics. *Nevertheless,* she conceded to his demands.

⁕ EXERCISE 9.18 ⁕

Underline the conjunctive adverbs in the following sentences.

1. We are vacationing in Orlando, Florida; however, we will not visit Universal Studios.
2. We could not escape through the doorways; hence, we used the fire escape.
3. Most people trust their doctors; nonetheless, they often seek second opinions.
4. You are a good person; nevertheless, I would not trust you with my life.
5. Writing a book takes a lot of patience; likewise, directing a movie does also.
6. She will not move in with me; moreover, she will not spend one night here.
7. I have to suffer the consequences; therefore, you cannot tell me what to do.
8. Some people believe in helping others; some, however, do not.
9. Stephen makes an excellent salary; on the other hand, he works more hours than most people.
10. Julia blames everyone for her misfortune; consequently, everyone stays away from her.

Insert conjunctive adverbs and the appropriate punctuation between the two complete thoughts in the following sentences. Write your answers above the sentences. Make any necessary changes in capitalization in the same way. Do not use any conjunctive adverb more than once.

1. The police officers broke the rules they were suspended.
2. Admitting that they are wrong is not easy for some people they pretend that they are right.
3. We did not mind helping her we had a good time.
4. Ruby lost her lottery ticket she was unable to claim her winnings.
5. Alex had never seen the Statue of Liberty he recognized it when we were in New York.
6. The physical therapist massaged my ankle it still hurts.
7. You aren't going to Panama with me you aren't going anywhere with me.
8. Many insurance companies are experiencing financial difficulties their rates are increasing.
9. Mary flunked the test Johnny flunked it.
10. I was disappointed that I did not receive the award I held my head high.

∽ **EXERCISE 9.20** ∾

Write 10 sentences containing conjunctive adverbs. Do not use any conjunctive adverb more than once.

1. _____
   _____
2. _____
   _____
3. _____
   _____
4. _____
   _____

5. _____

_____

6. _____

_____

7. _____

_____

8. _____

_____

9. _____

_____

10. _____

_____

❧ EXERCISE 9.21 ❧

*Underline the coordinating conjunctions, subordinating conjunctions, and conjunctive adverbs in the following selection. Above each, indicate whether it is a coordinating conjunction (**CC**), a subordinating conjunction (**SC**), or a conjunctive adverb (**CA**).*

It was cool on Saturday morning, yet the sun shone brightly against the windowpane of my Ford Taurus. I decided to take my usual trip to the flea market. I plowed through piles and piles of unneeded items. Suddenly, my eyes caught a glimpse of the most magnificent lamp. Golden hews sparkled from the glass globe adorned with brass flowers. Though I could not decide whether it would enhance my Old World furniture, it was beautiful just the same. So I thought, why not take a chance? The ticket hanging on the lamp read, "Dealer #73, golden lamp with brass flowers, $35." So I moved skillfully to the front counter and asked the dealer if she would negotiate the price, knowing that I would purchase it even if the price remained the same. The lady told me that she was not the owner, but she would call to check on a price that would be sufficient. In the meantime, I waited. After she placed the receiver on the telephone hook, she peered disdainfully at me and said that the owner would sell it to me for a mere $25. Although I did not want to appear too excited, the expression on my face must have told it all. I paid the money, plucked up my bargain, and strode jauntily out the front door.

‎ EXERCISE 9.22 ‎

*Underline the coordinating conjunctions, subordinating conjunctions, and conjunctive adverbs in the following selection. Above each, indicate whether it is a coordinating conjunction (**CC**), a subordinating conjunction (**SC**), or a conjunctive adverb (**CA**).*

A good driver anticipates what is to come. Therefore, the driver's eyes rove constantly from the road to the mirror to the car immediately ahead. The eyes also move from side to side, and they move as far ahead as they can readily see. Consequently, the driver always tries to be aware of the behavior of the traffic ahead in order to make adjustments. Flashing brake lights means that there is some obstruction of the flow of traffic. Cars edging into single lanes locate the obstruction for the driver. However, there is no indication as to whether the obstruction is caused by repair work or a stalled car. Swerving by many drivers ahead may mean that there is a bad pothole. But the absence of such signs does not promise clear traffic, and a good driver does not assume that it does. A driver who anticipates what is to come is rarely surprised by traffic conditions.

‎ EXERCISE 9.23 ‎

Underline the coordinating and subordinating conjunctions in the following selection.

Learning about World History

The Stone Age is a name used to describe a time when people used and relied on simple stone tools. The Stone Age is divided into the Old Stone Age, or Paleolithic Age, and the New Stone Age, or Neolithic Age.

Paleolithic people were nomads, people who moved in search of food. They lived by hunting, fishing, and gathering plants that grew wild. They followed herds of animals. If wild nuts or berries became scarce, they moved to another area where food was plentiful.

In the New Stone Age, people in many parts of the world gradually stopped hunting and gathering food and became farmers. They tamed wild animals such as sheep and goats and began to grow grain and vegetables for food. People grew crops that were suited to the local soil and climate.

Since people no longer had to move in search of food, they formed settlements, or villages. They began to build houses, and property became important. However, not everyone abandoned the nomadic way of life. Some people remained hunters and gatherers. Others herded sheep, goats, and cattle.

With the growth of the farming economy came the development of new technology. People began to use tools and skills to meet their basic needs. In the late Neolithic Age, people began to use metal as well as stone to make tools and weapons. They used copper first and eventually discovered that copper combined with tin formed a harder metal called bronze. People used the inventions of the late Neolithic Age to build more complex societies called civilizations.

❧ *10* ❧

Exclamation

DEFINING EXCLAMATION

An *exclamation* is a word or group of words used to express strong or sudden feelings, express emotions, or represent sounds. Most exclamations are followed by an exclamation point (!). Some exclamations express a relatively mild emotion; these should be set off by commas. Exclamatory sentences often omit elements that would normally be necessary for grammatical completeness.

Ouch! I hurt my back! (strong emotion)
Oh, I don't know. (mild emotion)
Splat! (sound)

Sometimes declarative (statement) sentences and interrogative (question) sentences show such strong feeling that they are more like exclamations than statements or questions. If so, the exclamation point should be used instead of the period or question mark:

You're awesome!
He finally finished reading the book!
Are you crazy!
Can't you see that I'm busy!

Add exclamations in the following sentences. Supply appropriate punctuation for each sentence. You may alter capitalization where necessary.

1. Show surprise

   _____ I didn't know that he was 70 years old

2. Show disappointment

   _____ I'll try again tomorrow

3. Show relief

   _____ What a relief

4. Show anger

   _____ You forgot to pick me up

5. Show happiness

   _____ He finally passed the entrance exam

6. Show hurt

   _____ That really hurts

7. Show compassion

   _____ I feel so sorry for you

8. Show excitement

   _____ Don't touch that button

9. Show disbelief

   _____ You're kidding

10. Show privacy

    _____ Don't let them hear you

Add exclamations and appropriate end punctuation in the following sentences.

1. _____ You closed the door on my hand

2. The stock market crashed again today

3. _____ Someone stole my purse

4. _____ She finally cleaned her room

5. I received a $10,000 raise today _____

6. _____ That car is coming straight into us

7. _____ It's a boy

8. I won the $43 million lottery _____

9. Don't ever embarrass me like that again _____

10. _____ That dress is beautiful

Review Test
Chapters 6–10

A. *Circle the adjectives, adverbs, and adjective and adverb phrases in the following sentences.*

1. Rome is well known for its breathtaking architectural buildings.

2. As it turned out, Morton was more dangerous than we imagined.

3. Darilyn moved awkwardly in the direction of her counterparts.

4. It is not very humid today.

5. The gray-haired, distinguished-looking man wore a bow tie to the sports event.

6. You received the appointment because you had an inside connection.

7. Registration for the fall semester begins tomorrow.

8. Small rodents stood on their hind legs and nibbled the tasty acorns.

9. At first glance, there is a striking similarity.

10. The huge plane landed roughly on the runway in Dallas, Texas.

B. *Underline the conjunctions, prepositions, and exclamations in the following sentences.*

1. Ouch! I burned my hand.

2. Turbulent thunderstorms in the eastern part of the United States were the worst in ten years.

3. The indigent man lay beside the tracks near the courthouse.

4. Kindness and courtesy are admirable traits.

5. Damon was completely mesmerized over the presidential elections.

6. It's all about the diamonds on her finger.

7. John put his key on the ledge above the door on the side of the cottage.

8. Near the top of the mountain, the daring climber fell onto the ground.

9. St. Martin has a French side and a Dutch side.

10. I'm tired of these shifting demands.

11. That injection hurt!

12. The building is designed to meet your needs and to also comply with the building code.

13. According to the records, James is neither rich nor poor.

14. The breaking news horrified the tenants, so they broke their leases.

15. Beyond the grove of trees stood five beautiful white stallions.

C. Underline the verbals and verbal phrases in the following sentences.

1. Both the husband and wife, being human beings, have their human frailties.

2. Bowling, swimming, and jogging keep my adrenaline flowing.

3. The teacher, devastated by the student's remark, struggled for words to explain her disappointment.

4. Screaming at the top of her voice, Gloria ran to safety.

5. To argue over trivial things is pointless.

6. Struggling to open the container, Jennifer's face turned beet red.

7. For over a decade, the attorney effectively represented his client.

8. Dining in exclusive Parisian restaurants proved to be quite invigorating.

9. Howling in the distance, the wild cat attacked its prey.

10. To continue at this pace would be detrimental to your mental and physical health.

❧ *11* ❧

Fragments

A *fragment* is an incomplete sentence that lacks a subject, a verb, or both. A fragment does not express a complete thought. The most common types of fragments are dependent-word fragments, added-detail fragments, *-ing* and *to* fragments, and missing-subject fragments.

DEPENDENT-WORD FRAGMENTS

Whenever you start a sentence with one of the following dependent words, there is a possibility that a fragment will result:

after	if	what, whatever
although	in order that	when, whenever
as	since	where, wherever
because	so that	whether
before	that	which, whichever
even if	though	while
even though	unless	who
how	until	whose

How to Correct a Dependent-Word Fragment

In most instances, you may correct a dependent-word fragment in one of three ways:

- By attaching the fragment to the sentence that comes before it

- By attaching the fragment to the sentence that comes after it

- By eliminating the dependent word and rewriting the sentence

If the dependent-word group comes at the beginning of a sentence, you must set it off with a comma.

Fragment: I will not complete this document. *Until you have read the first 50 pages.* (The second statement is a fragment because it does not make sense on its own. It needs the first sentence in order to make sense.)

Correction: I will not complete this document *until you have read the first 50 pages.*

Fragment: *Because he did not provide the details of the agreement.* I did not know what action to take. (The first statement is a fragment because it does not make sense on its own. It needs the second sentence in order to make sense.)

Correction: *Because he did not provide the details of the agreement,* I did not know what action to take.

Fragment: *When I decided to become an engineer.* I began to study day and night.

Correction: I decided to become an engineer and then began to study day and night. (The sentence was rewritten to eliminate the dependent word.)

Add a complete thought to each dependent-word group to make it a complete sentence. Use commas where necessary.

1. Because he hesitated when he saw me _____

   _____

   _____

2. Whenever Patricia's voice starts to quiver _____

   _____

   _____

3. Although they come from different ethnic backgrounds _____

   _____

   _____

4. The problems that we had _____

   _____

   _____

5. Even though he displayed confidence _____

   _____

   _____

6. Whether you like the instructions or not _____

   _____

   _____

7. Until I can see some improvement in your attitude _____

   _____

   _____

8. Before you begin to judge others _____

   _____

   _____

9. Whatever the possibilities are _____

   _____

10. We told the story many times _____

   _____

   _____

Underline the dependent-word group in each set. Correct each dependent-word group by attaching it to one of the other sentences. Insert commas and change capitalization where necessary.

1. The city was full of beautiful gothic buildings. That mesmerized the group. We plan to tour this area again next year.

2. After I shopped for my daughter's school clothes. I decided to purchase a few things for myself. Maybe I won't have to shop again until summer comes.

3. You will discover that the simple things in life are free. I've known this for a long time. When you realize that material things are not that important.

4. Since you have entertained several elite groups. You should be qualified to present a workshop on your experiences. All experiences are not the same.

5. Plain cakes tastes better. I think that I will cook one tomorrow. When ice cream and strawberries are added.

6. Before you claim too many dependents. Some people claim as many as 15! Be sure to consult a tax specialist.

7. His promotion is not imminent. He is a very thorough worker. Because he does not complete his tasks as scheduled.

8. Whenever you endeavor to do anything. All people do not have ambition. Do it well.

9. Because of the inequities of life. Some people give up. I don't know why they do this.

10. The building contractor gave them a bid. That they thought was ridiculous. They decided to look for someone whose bid was more reasonable.

ADDED-DETAIL FRAGMENTS

The added-detail fragment does not contain a subject or a verb. Added-detail fragments often begin with the words *also, especially, except, for example, including,* and *such as.*

How to Correct an Added-Detail Fragment

You can usually correct an added-detail fragment in one of three ways:

- Make the fragment a complete sentence by adding a subject and a verb.

- Attach the fragment to the sentence that comes before it.

- Change words as necessary to make the fragment part of the sentence that comes before it.

Fragment: I attend all of the recitals. *Including those that are not classical.*

Correction: I attend all of the recitals. *I even attend those that are not classical.*

Fragment: We enjoy playing cards. *Especially during the spring break.*

Correction: We enjoy playing cards, *especially during the spring break.*

Fragment: The philosopher provided his summation. *Also gave us handouts on his research.*

Correction: The philosopher provided his summation *and gave us handouts on his research.*

Fragment: I read The Great Gatsby. *The novel that my father liked so much.*

Correction: I read The Great Gatsby, *the novel that my father liked so much.*

Underline each added-detail fragment. Correct it by using one of the methods prescribed. Insert commas and change capitalization where necessary.

1. Heather enjoys attending college classes. Especially her chemistry class. She is the first person in class.
    (Add the fragment to the preceding sentence.)

2. She cooked the turkey and dressing the green beans. Also the potatoes. It was a delicious meal.
    (Change the words to make the fragment part of the preceding sentence.)

3. Reading is my favorite hobby. Especially reading science fiction. I go to the library every two weeks and check a book out.
    (Add a subject and a verb.)

4. He did not understand parts of the will. For example, the endowment. He decided to seek legal counsel.
    (Add a subject and a verb.)

5. All of the debts were paid. Except the ones that belonged to her husband. She felt that they were not her responsibility.
    (Add the fragment to the preceding sentence.)

6. We visited the ancient ruins. Also the modern buildings that were of interest. It was an unforgettable vacation.
    (Change the words to make the fragment part of the preceding sentence.)

7. The convention arena is filled with dignitaries. Especially senators and mayors. Perhaps this will be the best convention ever.
    (Add the fragment to the preceding sentence.)

8. The professors completed most of the course syllabi. Especially the developmental ones. All of them should be completed by next week.
    (Change the words to make the fragment part of the preceding sentence.)

9. He has an associate degree from Tarrant County College. Also a bachelor's degree from Prairie View A&M University. He is thinking about pursuing a master's degree.

(Add a subject and a verb.)

10. Don't interrupt me when I am talking. Especially if I am lecturing. It interferes with my concentration.

(Make the fragment part of the preceding sentence.)

-ING FRAGMENTS

When an -ing word appears at or near the start of a word group, a fragment may result. These fragments usually lack a subject and part of a verb.

How to Correct -ing Fragments

Most -ing fragments can be corrected in one of three ways:

- Attach the fragment to the sentence that comes before it or the sentence that comes after it. The sentence must make sense.

- Add a subject and change the -ing verb part to the correct verb form.

- Change being to the correct form of the verb be (is, are, was, were, am).

Fragment:	She sat by the telephone for hours. *Hoping to hear from him.*
Correction:	She sat by the telephone for hours, *hoping to hear from him.*

Fragment:	Gloria peered out of the window. *Not expecting what she saw.*
Correction:	Gloria peered out of the window. *She did not expect what she saw.*

Fragment:	I decided to stop reading the book. *It being difficult to comprehend.*
Correction:	I decided to stop reading the book. *It was difficult to comprehend.*

*Underline each -*ing *fragment and then correct it. Insert commas and change capitalization where necessary.*

1. We had a great time. Swimming in the crystal-clear water. We swam for several hours.
   (Attach the fragment to the sentence that comes before it.)

2. Hannah watched from the rear-view window. Not seeing the policeman. He parked his car behind her and gave her a ticket.
   (Add a subject and change the *-ing* verb part to the correct form of the verb.)

3. It being a very cloudy, dreary day. I lay in bed for most of the day. I took advantage of the opportunity to read a good book.
   (Change *being* to the correct form of the verb *be*.)

4. Trying to get ahead in life. Roderick works from early in the morning until late at night. He even works on weekends.
   (Attach the fragment to the sentence that comes after it.)

5. Attempting to broaden her horizons. She is studying music and dance. As a result, she will gain self-gratification.
   (Add a subject and change the *-ing* verb part to the correct form of the verb.)

6. I became very upset. Studying the details of the Civil War. My life will be changed forever.
   (Attach the fragment to the sentence that comes before it.)

7. Reading the book with much enthusiasm. I forgot that dinner was cooking in the oven. The family will be very upset.
   (Attach the fragment to the sentence that comes after it.)

8. She continued at the same pace. Not realizing the magnitude of the problem. Now she must suffer the consequences.
   (Add a subject and change the *-ing* verb part to the correct form of the verb.)

9. Many people have difficulty establishing credit. Establishing a good credit history is imperative. It being the key to obtaining the necessities as well as the luxuries of life.
   (Change *being* to the correct form of the verb *be*.)

10. I make it a practice to visit my mother often. Because she is very frail. She needs my undivided attention.
    (Attach the fragment to the sentence that comes after it.)

TO FRAGMENTS

A fragment sometimes results when *to* appears at or near the start of a word group.

How to Correct *to* Fragments

There are two ways to correct *to* fragments:

- Attach the fragment to the sentence that comes before it.
- Attach the fragment to the sentence that comes after it.

Fragment: Henry turned the corner quickly. *To avoid being seen.* He knew that he would be fired if his boss had seen him.

Correction: Henry turned the corner quickly *to avoid being seen.* He knew that he would be fired if his boss had seen him.

✣ *EXERCISE 11.5* ✣

Underline each to *fragment and then correct it by adding it to the sentence that comes before or after it. Insert commas and change capitalization where necessary.*

1. To impress his peers. David bought the most expensive tennis shoes in the store. Later, he regretted being so foolish.
2. He stepped up to the bench. To deny all charges placed against him. The judge was not pleased with his testimony.
3. The king was very reluctant. To relinquish his throne. However, he knew that he would have to.
4. David repaired the leaky faucet. To avoid having an extremely high water bill. His water bills are usually reasonable.
5. I completed the employment application. To avoid upsetting my parents. I want them to be proud of me.

MISSING-SUBJECT FRAGMENTS

Some fragments contain a verb but no subject.

How to Correct Missing-Subject Fragments

There are two ways to fix missing-subject fragments:

- Add a subject. You may use a pronoun that stands for the subject in the preceding sentence.
- Attach the fragment to the preceding sentence.

Fragment: Diaz prepares a budget. *But never uses it.* Maybe some day he will realize that budgets should be maintained.

Correction: Diaz prepares a budget. *But he never uses it.* Maybe some day he will realize that budgets should be maintained.

Correction: Diaz prepares a budget *but never uses it.* Maybe some day he will realize that budgets should be maintained.

✥ EXERCISE 11.6 ✥

Underline each missing-subject fragment. Then correct it.

1. She exercises for one hour each day. Then eats a large pizza. She defeats the purpose of exercising when she does not watch what she eats.

2. Alice despises Alicia. But pretends to be her friend. This is not the way to behave.

3. Cleaning a big house takes a lot of time. Easier if you plan ahead. That is what I always do.

4. Mother was detained in traffic. But arrived at her swimming class on time. She has never been late to her class.

5. We turned at the second intersection. Then got lost. Maybe we should have turned at the first intersection.

*Select the appropriate letter, either **a** or **b**, for the phrase that will make each of the following fragments into a meaningful complete sentence. Insert commas where necessary.*

1. After I finish installing the sprinkler
   system _____.

   a. I will landscape the yard
   b. circle the colors

2. To avoid being criticized _____.

   a. he conceded to her demands
   b. what you consider appropriate

3. Anxiously awaiting the trial _____.

   a. considered the circumstances
   b. he prepared his testimony

4. Even though the odds are against
   me _____.

   a. I will try anyway
   b. at the results

5. Albert Einstein and Eli Whitney _____.

   a. going to the convention
   b. were inventors

6. Pleading for leniency from the court _____.

   a. making an impression
   b. she presented her case

7. When you turn the switch on _____.

   a. turns the other way
   b. four bulbs light up

8. In July 1969, man walked _____.

   a. in the midstream of life
   b. on the moon for the first time

9. The earth is surrounded _____.

   a. by gases that make up the air
   b. water from all directions

10. The Watergate hearings will _____.

    a. never be forgotten
    b. remembered for years to come

*Select the appropriate letter, either **a** or **b**, for the phrase that will make each of the following fragments into a meaningful complete sentence. Insert commas where necessary.*

1. The moon is approximately _____.
   a. a quarter of a million miles from earth
   b. not at all

2. Taking every precaution not to disturb him _____.
   a. her soft-bottom shoes
   b. she tiptoed through

3. Sitting in the back seat _____.
   a. the pencil lay on the seat
   b. we laughed until we cried

4. Realizing that there was strong circumstantial evidence _____.
   a. the prosecutor did not
   b. the attorney presented her case with confidence

5. Never able to fulfill her ambition to become a doctor _____.
   a. self-image will deteriorate
   b. she simply gave up

6. The sun's rays on that hot, humid day in the middle of the summer _____.
   a. were excruciatingly painful
   b. likely to get worse

7. Across the river and around the bend _____.
   a. the well-written paper
   b. pranced the beautiful horse

8. Swimming in the crystal-clear water _____.
   a. brought back special memories
   b. like a fish

9. Unless we had read the play *The Glass Menagerie* _____.
   a. we forfeited our recess period
   b. we also read *The Shoes of the Fisherman*

10. Realizing that he had committed the ultimate crime _____.
    a. he ran for safety
    b. during a moment of passion

Correct each of the dependent-word groups by adding a complete thought. Insert commas where necessary.

1. Because he did not understand the directions _____ _____.

2. Determined to take matters into his own hands _____ _____.

3. Watching the miniseries late at night _____ _____.

4. _____ all night long the day before yesterday.

5. _____ disappeared into the night.

6. Until he learns to obey _____ _____.

7. _____ _____ asking too many questions.

8. _____ my favorite president.

9. Because of a lack of self-control _____ _____.

10. If you slam that door again _____ _____.

11. Making the answers very clear _____ _____.

12. _____ painting her portrait.

13. While calculating his expenses _____ _____.

14. _____ explained the details of the contract.

15. Since you will not promise to keep the secret _____

_____ .

16. _____ cried until someone

came to rescue her puppy.

17. As Mr. Oyegoke entered the front gate _____

_____ .

18. _____

are Mattie and Tanya.

19. Chances are _____

_____ .

20. The accountant's yearly income _____

_____ .

∽ 12 ∾

Run-Ons

A *run-on* occurs when two complete sentences run together without a clear break between them. Run-ons that have no break at all between thoughts are called *fused sentences*. Run-ons in which only a comma separates the two complete thoughts are called *comma splices*.

Run-On: My daughter attended the Oak Hills Academy I was not very impressed with it.

How to Correct a Run-On

There are four options for correcting a run-on:

- Use a comma plus a joining word (the coordinating conjunction *and, but, for, or, nor, so,* or *yet*) to connect the two complete thoughts.
- Use a period and a capital letter to break the two thoughts into separate sentences.
- Use a semicolon to join the complete thoughts.
- Use a transition (conjunction or conjunctive adverb) to join the complete thoughts. (See Chapter 9.)

Corrections

My daughter attended Oak Hills Academy, but I was not very impressed with it.

My daughter attended Oak Hills Academy. I was not very impressed with it.

My daughter attended Oak Hills Academy; I was not very impressed with it.

My daughter attended Oak Hills Academy; however, I was not very impressed with it.

Correct each run-on by putting a comma and a joining word between the two complete thoughts.

1. I own two mink coats I no longer wear them because I fear animal activists.

2. The majority of my time and energy is devoted to practicing it will pay off in the near future.

3. Procrastination is a dangerous thing it can cause many problems.

4. The likelihood of having twins is very slim twins do not run in our family.

5. I always meet my goals this makes me wonder whether I set them high enough.

6. People say that "absence makes the heart grow fonder" this is not always a true statement.

7. Many people wish to become wealthy all I seek is to maintain a comfortable lifestyle.

8. The overwhelming evidence led to a conviction there was no way that he could avoid being sentenced.

9. Satellite television is a great invention I believe that it has thwarted communication within families.

10. I've read many great books *Testimony of Two Men* by Taylor Caldwell is my favorite.

❧ **EXERCISE 12.2** ❧

Correct each run-on by making it into two separate sentences. Capitalize where necessary.

1. Escada and Ellen Tracy are considered high-quality clothing brands there are others that are just as good.

2. I have strong convictions concerning certain issues I am nonchalant concerning others.

3. They are avid filmgoers they never have time to visit with their neighbors.

4. Car accidents occur several times each day they are not as dangerous as airplane trips.

5. Sticks and stones may break my bones words will never hurt me.

6. Several articles of clothing were left in the bag we will donate them to Goodwill Industries if the owner does not claim them.

7. Chances are you will submit your paper late you will lose 10 points from your final grade if you do.

8. Van Cliburn will perform at Bass Performance Hall in June he is a great pianist.

9. Businesses are popping up all over town a lot of others are closing their doors.

10. My husband has no problem with polishing silver he hates to wash dishes.

✣ EXERCISE 12.3 ✤

Correct each run-on by placing a semicolon between the two thoughts.

1. California Cooper is a writer she lives in Texas.
2. The lily is a beautiful flower, the rose is magnificent.
3. The novels are on the top shelf the periodicals are on the bottom shelf.
4. Box seats cost more than the seats on the floor I will settle for the floor.
5. Roberta stirred the cake with all of her might her sister looked on in awe.
6. The stock market fell 10 percent in the first quarter my father lost a lot of money.
7. Airplanes soar thousands of feet into the sky, they provide the fastest mode of transportation.
8. Peculiar things happen whenever she comes around we try to avoid her.
9. Bread and butter go together ice cream and pickles do not.
10. One friend is better than thousands of acquaintances, you are a true friend.

EXERCISE 12.4

Correct each run-on in a way that makes sense. You may use commas and conjunctions, periods, semicolons, or conjunctive adverbs. Capitalize where necessary, and punctuate appropriately.

1. Hai lives in Bristow, Virginia, Tie lives in Houston, Texas.
2. Mr. Levy's tests are very difficult Mrs. O'Reilly's tests are too easy.
3. The sun is 93 million miles away from the earth that is a long distance.
4. Edgar Allan Poe is one of my favorite writers he led a strange life.
5. He lived as if there were no tomorrow, now he is flat broke.
6. Socrates was a famous Greek philosopher, Plato was also very popular.
7. The computer monitor is too small there is not enough space on the hard drive.
8. Heather turned in her nomination form she thought there would be two winners.
9. Dominique wrote a book she looked forward to receiving her first royalty check.
10. He was proved guilty, the judge was very lenient.

EXERCISE 12.5

Correct each run-on in a way that makes sense. You may use commas and conjunctions, periods, semicolons, or conjunctive adverbs. Capitalize where necessary, and punctuate appropriately.

1. The chair matched the sofa the ottoman was an odd piece.
2. She used all of her resources he did not contribute a thing.
3. Gertrude lay at the edge of the lake she daydreamed about her future.
4. The Oriental rug is multicolored it matches her décor perfectly.
5. Victor is the CEO of the corporation Isaac is the president.
6. Twenty-five percent of her money is invested in stocks the rest is invested in bonds.
7. A wise person thinks before acting a foolish person does not.
8. The stones tumbled from the mountaintop, we ran to avoid being hit.
9. Capital punishment is a controversial issue I do not know what stand to take.
10. Practice every day and you will succeed do nothing and you will fail.

TRANSITIONS

As noted in Chapter 9, conjunctions and conjunctive adverbs can describe the relationship between thoughts as we move (transition) from one thought to the next. Here are some examples of the types of relationships that can be conveyed by various words and phrases used as transitions.

Relationship	Transitions		
Time	afterward	after a few days	meanwhile
	at last	again	before
	first	in the beginning	suddenly
	second	at length	finally
	soon	during	next
	concurrently	shortly thereafter	immediately
	subsequently	in the meantime	while
	then	at the same time	at the start
Addition	equally important	next	moreover
	then, too	also	and
	first of all	as well as	besides
	furthermore	first	again
	still another	not only . . . but also	in addition
Place	under	behind	on top of
	near	above	opposite
	adjacent to	nearby	far from
	below	farther away	in the distance
	over	beyond	
Contrast	unlike	in contrast	however
	but	after all	still
	yet	or	nevertheless
	on the contrary	on the other hand	nor
Comparison	just as	similar to	likewise
	like	identical to	similarly

Relationship	Transitions		
Cause and effect	thus	hence	after
	subsequently	consequently	as a result
	therefore	therefore	accordingly
Conclusion	thus	consequently	finally
	therefore	in conclusion	last of all
	in summary	as a result	then
Repetition	again	as has been noted	to be sure
	as I have said	in other words	
Example	for example	for instance	such as
	in this instance		
Purpose	with this objective	for this purpose	to this end
Emphasis	in fact	in any event	indeed

❧ EXERCISE 12.6 ❧

Fill each blank with a transition that makes sense. Use a semicolon before the transition and a comma after it. Do not use any transition more than once.

1. Her memory is not very good _____ she retains the things that are important to her.

2. I cooked macaroni and cheese yesterday _____ I cooked spinach.

3. You may not use my car _____ you may not ride with me.

4. Sarah must enroll in college in three months _____ she must get a part-time job.

5. He has never been out of the state of Texas _____ he is very knowledgeable about the American states.

6. You must reciprocate every favor that I do for you _____ start doing so immediately.

7. The grass is not always greener on the other side _____ take the bird in the hand instead of the two in the bush.

8. My aunt is a green-eyed monster _____ she has no friends.

9. The tile squares sparkled brightly _____ Jennifer was recognized for her hard work.

10. I will not concede to your demands _____ I will pretend not to hear them.

⨾ EXERCISE 12.7 ⨽

Indicate in the blank whether each sentence is a comma splice (CS), a fused sentence (FS), or correct (OK). Correct the faulty sentences.

_____ 1. Physics is a very difficult subject, English is very easy.

_____ 2. I'm cooking the dinner myself I know that it will be a disaster.

_____ 3. James Baldwin wrote *Go Tell It on the Mountain*, Charles Dickens wrote *David Copperfield*.

_____ 4. He has traveled the same route for the past 20 years.

_____ 5. Mark is a computer analyst, Marie is an Internet engineer.

_____ 6. Captain John Paul Jones said, "I have not yet begun to fight," Benjamin Mays said, "The man who outthinks you rules you."

_____ 7. The fax machine belongs to me the scanner belongs to my sister.

_____ 8. It takes a lot of determination to complete a college degree it takes even more determination to complete a second one.

_____ 9. He wrote an autobiography we think that most of the details are untrue.

_____ 10. The Waterford crystal was beautiful, the Lenox china enhanced it.

EXERCISE 12.8

Indicate in the blank whether each sentence is a comma splice (CS), a fused sentence (FS), or correct (OK). Correct the faulty sentences.

_____ 1. Virginia taught Economics II for two years she taught Business Law I for five years.

_____ 2. I noticed the stain yesterday when I was washing.

_____ 3. The bride was 30 minutes late the groom did not show up at all.

_____ 4. Hannah loses weight easily, her friend does not.

_____ 5. Troy swims three times a day he is an avid swimmer.

_____ 6. Paul never thought much about the situation.

_____ 7. The savings bond matured we still did not have enough money.

_____ 8. I wish that I could turn back the hands of time.

_____ 9. *The Grapes of Wrath* by John Steinbeck is an excellent novel.

_____ 10. California is located on the West Coast I live on the East Coast.

❧ *13* ❧

Dangling and Misplaced Modifiers

DANGLING MODIFIERS

A *dangling modifier* is a modifying phrase or clause that does not clearly and sensibly modify a word in the sentence. When a modifying phrase containing a verbal (see Chapter 6) comes at the beginning of a sentence, the phrase is followed by a comma. Immediately after that comma should come the word that the word group modifies.

As you practice using different kinds of sentences that will reflect the turns of your thinking, you may find yourself sometimes writing dangling modifiers. *Do not* allow the recurrence of dangling modifiers to discourage you from further experiments in your writing. You cannot learn to handle new tools skillfully without practice. Instead of being discouraged, learn how to avoid dangling modifiers and how to recognize and correct them when they do occur.

Dangling modifier:	*After talking on the phone,* dinner was served. (This sentence seems to say that dinner talked on the phone.)
Correction:	After talking on the telephone, *I served dinner.*
Dangling modifier:	*While riding the bicycle,* the cold wind hit my face. (This sentence seems to say that the wind was riding the bicycle.)
Correction:	While *I was* riding the bicycle, the cold wind hit my face.

As you can see, dangling modifiers are corrected by either revising the sentence or by adding words to make the meaning logical and clear.

Write complete sentences using the following introductory modifiers. Be sure that each modifier is followed by a word that it can clearly and sensibly modify.

1. Crying unexpectedly, _____

   _____

   _____

2. Disturbed by John's remark, _____

   _____

   _____

3. Flitting from flower to flower, _____

   _____

   _____

4. Walking along the beach, _____

   _____

   _____

5. Rubbing his face, _____

   _____

   _____

6. Not expecting the bad news, _____

   _____

   _____

7. Surfing the Internet, _____

   _____

   _____

8. Screening all applicants, _____

   _____

   _____

9. To avoid being caught, _____

   _____

   _____

10. Trying to keep the peace, _____

   _____

   _____

Eliminate the dangling modifiers in the following sentences by rewriting each sentence so that each modifier clearly and sensibly modifies a word in the sentence. Words may need to be supplied.

1. Driving around the corner, the curb was nearly run over.

   _____

   _____

2. Immediately after finishing school, my bank account was exhausted.

   _____

   _____

3. After having heart surgery, recovery was expected to take several months.

   _____

   _____

4. While singing loudly, the dog ran into the living room.

   _____

   _____

5. Being tired, the park bench looked inviting.

   _____

   _____

6. While negotiating the contract, the briefcase containing the important papers flew open suddenly.

   _____

   _____

7. Before going to bed, the lights are turned off.

   _____

   _____

8. After reading the speeding citation, the car was parked in the garage.

   _____

   _____

9. Dancing to the music of the '60s, the records sounded fantastic.

   _____

   _____

10. While fidgeting with the matches, my hair was burned.

   _____

   _____

*Several of the following sentences contain dangling modifiers. If a sentence is correct, write **OK** before the number. If the sentence is incorrect, write **DM** before the number. Correct each dangling modifier sentence by rewriting it on the blank lines below the sentence.*

_____ **1.** After eating the delicious appetizer, the lunch was a disappointment.

_____

_____

_____ **2.** Anticipating a bad report, I was a nervous wreck.

_____

_____

_____ **3.** Typing at a fast pace, the old typewriter broke.

_____

_____

_____ **4.** While working in the garden, a wasp stung me.

_____

_____

_____ **5.** Setting the clocks in the building, dust fell everywhere.

_____

_____

_____ **6.** Running in the cul-de-sac, my ankle was sprained.

_____

_____

_____ **7.** While changing the tire, sweat trickled down my face.

_____

_____

_____ **8.** Golfing early in the day, a prairie dog popped up on the sixth fairway.

_____

_____

_____ 9. Sitting at my desk, the light shined brightly.

_____

_____

_____ 10. Turning in a clockwise motion, the cap finally came off the fruit jar.

_____

_____

✣ EXERCISE 13.4 ✣

Eliminate the dangling modifiers in the following sentences by rewriting each sentence.

1. Strolling down Sunset Boulevard, the architecture of the buildings impressed me.

_____

_____

2. Being very hungry, this quiche looks as good as fried chicken to me.

_____

_____

3. After working all day, a shower is refreshing.

_____

_____

4. While reading a good book by the river, the wind started to blow ferociously.

_____

_____

5. Bumping along in the jeep, the sunset looked beautiful.

_____

_____

6. Immediately after washing the clothes, the doorbell rang.

_____

_____

7. Jingling the coins in my purse, the clasp came off and fell to the floor.

_____

_____

8. While flying into San Francisco, the Golden Gate Bridge came into view.

_____

_____

9. Stepping on the brakes, the car skidded.

_____

_____

10. Being literate, this refresher course is unnecessary.

_____

_____

MISPLACED MODIFIERS

A _misplaced modifier_ is a modifier that does have something in the sentence to modify, but it is put in the wrong place so that it seems to modify something that you do not mean to modify. The essential difference between a dangling modifier and a misplaced modifier is that a dangling modifier cannot fit logically anywhere in the sentence. With the misplaced modifier, the modifier merely does not belong where it is placed in the sentence and needs to be moved.

Remember that for clarity, modifiers should go as close as possible to the elements they modify. Correcting a misplaced modifier is easy: move it from the confusing position and put it where it will be clear. Sometimes you may need to rephrase the whole sentence, but most often you need merely to rearrange it.

Misplaced modifier:	Five freshmen were punished after the rules were broken _by the principal_.
Correction:	Five freshmen were punished _by the principal_ after the rules were broken.

The following sentences contain misplaced modifiers. Rewrite the sentences so that they make sense.

1. Spot enjoyed the chunks of steak slipped to him by the guests under the table.

_____

_____

2. A lovely rose garden was planted by my husband behind the fence.

_____

_____

3. On the bottom shelf of the pantry, I did not see the crackers.

_____

_____

4. There is a postcard written by my cousin Indira in your mailbox.

_____

_____

5. The club sent a sympathy card to the relatives of the dead man in a hurry.

_____

_____

6. The dedicated teacher told the children what they were doing wrong with a smile.

_____

_____

7. In a tiny cage at the dog pound, my grandchildren felt very sorry for the little chow.

_____

_____

8. Did you read about the president who was impeached in this morning's paper?

_____

_____

9. Confined in a small cage, we pitied the huge animal.

_____

_____

10. While eating his dog food, dad noticed that the poodle seemed very hungry.

_____

_____

The following sentences contain misplaced modifiers. Rewrite the sentences so that they make sense.

1. The frightened teenagers fled out the back door involved in the altercation.

   _____

   _____

2. Females have difficulty climbing the fence wearing dresses.

   _____

   _____

3. The master of ceremonies presented the award eating cheesecake.

   _____

   _____

4. Pat joined the football team weighing 120 pounds.

   _____

   _____

5. Using a new tool, the audio system was installed in the car.

   _____

   _____

6. I noticed many new businesses driving down Madison Avenue.

   _____

   _____

7. My daughter attended the beauty school taking six hours per semester.

   _____

   _____

8. The articulate spokesperson delivered her speech wearing horn-rimmed glasses.

   _____

   _____

9. His father decided to teach him to drive on the day he was born.

   _____

   _____

10. While marching on the football field, the spectators yelled loudly.

   _____

   _____

*The following sentences contain dangling and misplaced modifiers. Rewrite the sentences to make the meanings clear. In the blank before the number, write **DM** for dangling modifier or **MM** for misplaced modifier.*

_____ 1. Mother served spaghetti to Karen and me, loaded with garlic and tomato sauce.

_____

_____

_____ 2. Waiting for the latest news forecast, the television broke.

_____

_____

_____ 3. After boiling for eight minutes, my aunt put the potatoes in the strainer.

_____

_____

_____ 4. Trying to remember my lines, my heart pounded furiously.

_____

_____

_____ 5. After eating 50 finger sandwiches, the hostess asked us to save some for the other guests.

_____

_____

_____ 6. Although very well constructed, Midori lives in an old, antiquated house.

_____

_____

_____ 7. Before leaving work, my computer drawings were perfect.

_____

_____

_____ 8. After cooking dinner, the telephone rang.

_____

_____

_____ **9.** Flying at half-mast, my heart grew sad when I saw the flag.

_____

_____

_____ **10.** A dead turtle was brought into camp by a Girl Scout 12 inches long.

_____

_____

✿ EXERCISE 13.8 ✿

The following sentences contain dangling and misplaced modifiers. Rewrite the sentences to make the meanings clear. In the blank before the number, write **DM** for dangling modifier or **MM** for misplaced modifier.

_____ **1.** After spending two weeks fishing in the mountains, the office seemed very confining.

_____

_____

_____ **2.** Jesus and I waited for you until the movie started at the theater entrance.

_____

_____

_____ **3.** Howling through the treetops, I could hear the wind.

_____

_____

_____ **4.** After fighting the last bout, the referee announced the winner.

_____

_____

_____ **5.** We found an old record player in the backyard that would not work.

_____

_____

_____ 6. The first person to see the wild animal, a veterinary student from Sweden, was Aman Gaut.

_____

_____

_____ 7. The living room suite was very beautiful that they bought at Gabbert's.

_____

_____

_____ 8. While playing the music, the dogs ran through the house and yelped loudly.

_____

_____

_____ 9. The chemist called it sulfuric acid who examined the substance in the flask.

_____

_____

_____ 10. On cycling closer, the animal took a great leap onto my head.

_____

_____

14

Parallelism

Parallelism, or parallel form, is putting similar ideas together in similar form. Parallelism requires that two or more similar words, phrases, or clauses that serve the same function be presented in exactly the same way. Comprehension is increased through the use of skillfully repeated patterns; this makes parallelism an important device for writing effective sentences.

Not parallel: Mark enjoys jogging, singing, and to dance.

Parallel: Mark enjoys jogging, singing, and dancing.

Not parallel: The children hopped, skipped, and jump all the way to the store.

Parallel: The children hopped, skipped, and jumped all the way to the store.

Not parallel: He ran down the stairs, out the front door, and rushed into the street.

Parallel: He ran down the stairs, flew out the front door, and rushed into the street.

Parallel: He ran down the stairs, out the front door, and into the street.

Not parallel: She wore a beautiful hairstyle, a lovely dress, and her shoes were fashionable.

Parallel: She wore a beautiful hairstyle, a lovely dress, and fashionable shoes.

*Each group has one item that does not match the others in parallel form. Change each incorrect item to parallel form. Write the correct answers in the blank. Two word groups are correct. Write **OK** if the words in the group are parallel.*

1. basking in the sun, swimming in the lake, at the spectators _____
2. fish, swimming, bowling _____
3. beautiful paintings, quaint houses, restaurants _____
4. around the barn, through the meadow, the hill _____
5. smiling, jumped, laughed _____
6. up-to-date movies, out-of-date book, dead-end street _____
7. typist, journalist, guitarist _____
8. articulating, intelligent, witty _____
9. prompt, dependable, courtesy _____
10. economically, politically, physical _____

PARALLELISM USING PAIRED EXPRESSIONS

Certain paired expressions require that parallel forms follow each half of the pair. Some of the most common paired expressions are *both . . . and, not only . . . but also, rather . . . than, either . . . or,* and *neither . . . nor.*

Both dieting *and* exercising are excellent ways to lose weight.

Writing academic books is *not only* time-consuming *but also* nerve-racking.

I would *rather* ride on a plane *than* drive in a car.

Either the part is faulty *or* it is installed improperly.

She is *neither* pretty *nor* ugly.

Supply the words needed to form parallel paired constructions in the following sentences.

1. He would *rather* die _____ live without her.

2. *Neither* buying me expensive jewelry _____ taking me on wonderful vacations will change my mind.

3. Derrick is *both* inquisitive _____ intelligent.

4. This is *not only* the most difficult course that I have ever taken _____ the most interesting.

5. The attorney is *either* procrastinating _____ preparing for the defense.

6. *Both* Jane _____ Ida arrived late.

7. Clarence and Karen Randles said that they would *rather* purchase a Ford Expedition _____ a Ford Explorer.

8. I find *both* playing the piano _____ playing the organ to be easy.

9. You are _____ my mother *nor* my guardian.

10. You will *either* do as I say _____ suffer the consequences.

Rewrite the following sentences to put them in parallel form.

1. After the plane took off, the passengers talked, watched movies, read, and were sleeping.

   _____

   _____

2. Both Fran but also Candy were a little crazy.

   _____

   _____

3. He was neither happy or sad.

_____

_____

4. The telephone repairmen are working in either my back yard nor yours.

_____

_____

5. The Calvary went across the river and the hills.

_____

_____

6. Neither the dean or the professor would approve the student's reinstatement.

_____

_____

7. Either you will concede to his demands nor move into another apartment.

_____

_____

8. You are not only selfish but disrespectful.

_____

_____

9. I would rather attend the concert instead of going to the movies.

_____

_____

10. Jessica is not only talented but resourceful.

_____

_____

❧ EXERCISE 14.4 ❧

The following selection is not a complete paragraph. Underline the parallel structures. Use a different type of underlining for each parallel set (for example, straight line, wavy line, double line, dotted line).

Some choose to become attorneys who win big cases that will make them rich, famous, and recognized all over the world. Some choose to become doctors who cure ailments, alleviate aches and pains, and save lives. Some choose to become chemists who concoct chemical formulas through the composition and transformation of substances. Some choose to become gemologists who specialize in the identification and classification of gemstones, ranging from the lowest to the highest in quality, identifying the clarity, color, weight, and cut of each gemstone. Some choose to become architects who design huge structures that fascinate the multitudes.

∽ *15* ⋍

Punctuation

COMMAS

Commas in a Series

- In sentences that contain three or more parallel parts, such as words, phrases, or short clauses (see Chapter 14), place a comma after each part except the last. Be sure to place a comma before the conjunction.

  > The items needed for the presentation are *paper, pens,* and *pencils.*
  >
  > The interior decorator was told to *reupholster the sofa and loveseat, change the color of the wallpaper,* and *order new furniture.*
  >
  > *Paul changed the ink cartridge, Jessica typed the manuscript,* and *I inserted the pictures.*

- Note that commas are *not* used when parallel parts in a series are *all* joined by conjunctions:

  > Ming enjoys *golfing* and *bowling* and *bicycling.*

- Sometimes *etc.* is used to indicate "and so forth" at the end of a series. When *etc.* is used, it is set off by commas and is never preceded by the word *and:*

  > Hortense ordered fabric, cornice boards, fringe, *etc.,* for her new draperies.

- Use a comma before an ampersand (&) in organizational names only if the organization officially uses the comma in its name:

> He worked for *Gorham, Peters & James.*
>
> Did he accept the position of presidency at *Yancy, Bates, & Reyes?*

Commas with Adjectives in Series

- Two equally important adjectives not connected by *and* should be separated with a comma:

> The new show is a *funny, intelligent* production suitable for viewers of all ages.

Commas in Apposition

- When something is restated in different words, the restatement is an *appositive* and is set off by commas (see Chapter 6).

> Our next-door neighbor, *Mr. Rutkosky,* repairs small appliances.
>
> The family pet, *a purebred keeshond,* won first prize at the dog show last spring.

- When a restated name or item is one-of-a-kind, it is set off with commas. If the name or item is one of several possibilities, it is not set off with commas.

> My brother, *Jarred,* is a medical doctor. [Jarred is my only brother.]
>
> My brother *Jarred* is a medical doctor. [I have more than one brother; the one named Jarred is a medical doctor.]
>
> Her novel, *Life in the Slow Lane,* was a best-seller. [This is the only novel she has written.]
>
> Her novel *Life in the Slow Lane* was a best-seller, but her latest one was a flop.

- Reflexive pronouns are not considered appositives and are not set off with commas.

> You all seem so full of energy, but I *myself* am quite tired today.

Commas in Dates and Time Zones

- Calendar date, year date, and weekday combinations require commas:

     Our older son graduated from college on May 9, 2000.

     Our younger son will graduate from college on Saturday, May 8, 2004.

- Commas may or may not be used in expressions of month and year, but consistency must be maintained throughout the text:

     Acceptable: *July 2005* is the deadline for submitting applications.

     Acceptable: *July, 2005,* is the deadline for submitting applications.

- Use commas to set off a time zone used with clock times:

     The flight will leave Washington Dulles Airport at 10:30 a.m., EST.

Commas with Place Names

- In a sentence, use a comma to set off the city from the state and a comma after the state:

     His home in Bastrop, Texas, is very plush.

Commas with Independent Clauses and Dependent Clauses

- A comma is used to separate two independent clauses joined by a coordinating conjunction (see Chapter 9). The words that follow the conjunction must form a complete sentence:

     The introduction to the United States Constitution is rather lengthy, but the Preamble is relatively short.

- A dependent clause used to provide an extra idea or comment within a sentence is nonrestrictive and may be set off with commas:

     We will, *if time permits,* take a 15-minute break.

Commas after Introductory Words, Clauses, and Phrases

- A comma is used to separate a dependent clause from an independent (main) clause when the dependent clause is introductory. Some introductory words are *if, as, because, when, since, after, although, before, provided, so, unless, until, whenever,* and *while.*

    Since I started taking the recommended dietary supplement, I have felt well.
    As agreed, we will continue this discussion in the privacy of our home.

- Nonrestrictive clauses and phrases that supply additional information but do not change the meaning of the sentence should be set off with commas:

    The article, *which appeared in yesterday's paper,* was astonishing.

Commas with Direct Address

- The name of a person being addressed directly, or a title used in lieu of that name, should be set off with commas:

    Thanks for all your help with the wedding, *Pete.*
    We are thrilled, *Doctor,* that you have joined our staff.

Commas with Degrees and Abbreviations

- College degrees and abbreviations reflecting corporate status that appear after names are set off with commas:

    Terri Forte, *Ph.D.,* is the president of Oakland Manor Golf Club.
    Fell & Fell, *Inc.,* will represent him concerning the company's legal problems.

Commas with Quotations

- Direct quotations should always be set off with commas:

    Thurgood Marshall said, "I believe in gradualism, but 90-odd years is gradual enough."

"I believe in gradualism, but 90-odd years is gradual enough," said Thurgood Marshall.

"I believe in gradualism," said Thurgood Marshall, "but 90-odd years is gradual enough."

- If a stronger punctuation mark (such as a dash or a question mark) is present, the comma should be omitted:

    "The result"—highly unexpected, I might add—"was a whole new class of polymers."

    "Why do I love you?" she mused. "That's an easy question!" she said with a laugh.

Commas with Complimentary Closings

- The complimentary closing in a letter should end with a comma:

    Sincerely yours,   Yours truly,   Best regards,

✌ EXERCISE 15.1 ✌

Insert commas where necessary in the following sentences.

1. Mrs. Smith the guest artist prepared an impressive display.
2. Please pass me the peas potatoes and bread.
3. The book is attractive informative and controversial.
4. She begged the domineering meticulous assistant but she was unable to dissuade her.
5. I went scuba diving last week but I'm not eager to go again.
6. Jim Thorne who lives on the North Side asked for the opportunity to show his skill.
7. Our first annual family reunion is scheduled for Wednesday July 12 2004.
8. Realizing that she was not prepared for the recital she feigned illness.
9. "Thanks a million David for bathing my poodle" she said.
10. Ling planned my trip purchased my ticket and drove me to the airport.

Insert commas where necessary in the following sentences.

1. The birdwatcher said "That is a bluejay nesting in the live oak tree."

2. The two of them Mr. Washington and Professor Yallow arrived after the dedication.

3. The volunteers from the three schools (Bonner Madison and Parr) worked all day putting the project together.

4. On the other hand we did qualify for a personal loan.

5. Werger Brant & Eghart proposed a business plan that would benefit all of the companies.

6. The five young women simultaneously asked "What does it cost?"

7. In the meantime discontinue use of the prescribed medicine.

8. Paul Marie and Shamika are claims adjusters.

9. The three branches of government are the executive legislative and judicial branches.

10. "Let's get this party started!" shrieked the energetic loud-voiced entertainer.

Insert commas where necessary in the following sentences.

1. A lot of talented ambitious people entered the contest.

2. "The problem" intoned Mr. Joyce "is that over half of the staff was late this morning."

3. It has been many many years since the catering service opened in his father's name.

4. Mitchell A. Parks M.D. became a volunteer fireman after he retired.

5. As agreed Jane and Wong will write the article within one month.

6. The three decided all things considered to accept the changes without delay.

7. We added two new subjects to our curriculum last year; this year three.

8. The father not the mother decided where the children would attend school.

9. The personal trainer purchased new treadmills bicycles and weights.

10. The seven continents are Europe Asia Africa Antarctica North America South America and Australia.

SEMICOLONS

- A *semicolon* is used to separate independent clauses of a compound sentence when a conjunction is omitted:

  Conquetta passed the English test, *but* she failed the chemistry test. (The conjunction *but* is used.)

  Conquetta passed the English test; she failed the chemistry test. (No conjunction is used.)

- If items in a series contain internal commas, separate the items with semicolons:

  The base colors are brown, mauve, and taupe; the trim colors are cream, beige, and eggplant; and the carpet is a deep, rich blue.

  We vacationed in Orlando, Florida; Knoxville, Tennessee; and Nashville, Tennessee.

  Dr. Julienne, our principal, is out of her office today; Dr. Jacquette, the vice president, will be in charge.

- When joining independent clauses, conjunctive adverbs and transitions (see Chapters 9 and 12) are preceded by a semicolon and followed by a comma:

  The results of the DNA tests were inconclusive; *therefore,* the jury had no logical reason to find him guilty.

- A semicolon at the end of a quotation goes outside the quotation marks:

  Lerone Bennett Jr. stated, "Violence always rebounds, always returns home"; the audience listened attentively.

COLONS

- Colons are used to introduce explanatory statements or lists:

  Cleo explained her situation: she was late for work because she overslept.

- A colon should be used only at the end of an independent clause (complete sentence):

Incorrect:	The Boy Scouts asked for: backpacks, pocket knives, and mosquito repellent.
Correct:	The Boy Scouts asked for backpacks, pocket knives, and mosquito repellent.
Correct:	The Boy Scouts asked for the following items: backpacks, pocket knives, and mosquito repellent.

- Use a colon between the title and subtitle of a book or article:

  Punctuation Made Easy: A Comprehensive Handbook

- In literary references, use a colon between the place of publication and the name of the publisher in footnotes or endnotes:

  Los Angeles: Star Books, 2001.

Insert semicolons and colons where necessary in the following sentences.

1. Four best-selling books were purchased however, no one read them.
2. Among those competing were Judy Scrup, Belleville High School Clarence Taylor, Hogan High School and Pete Latimer, Troup High School.
3. The bulletin board displayed the names of the winners this was a great idea.
4. The payroll checks were not printed before lunch today therefore, I was unable to pay my rent.
5. Ours will become one of the most advertised products in the nation it will be seen via television, it will stand tall on billboards, it will be advertised in the newspapers, and it will ring out from radio stations.
6. Our itinerary requires the following stops Turkey, Italy, and Greece.
7. He didn't leave the premises when the fire alarm sounded on the contrary, he started talking on the telephone.
8. Success in the cosmetics industry requires the following a nose for fragrances, a flair for makeup application, and experience in product research.
9. Dr. Martin Luther King was a civil rights activist he demonstrated the nonviolent approach in resolving delicate issues.
10. Ronnie explained the process for painting a house the painters need to make long, quick strokes across the wooden boards.

QUOTATION MARKS

- A direct quotation is the exact wording used by a speaker or writer. Direct quotations should be placed within quotation marks:

"You must," said Mr. Rothmier, "complete this painting by noon today."

- Use quotation marks around the titles of short works, such as articles in magazines, newspapers, or books; short stories; chapters in a book; songs; and poems:

> Payton read the article "How to Lose 10 Pounds in Two Days."
> "The Innocent Man" is my favorite short story.
> Professor Yank read the first chapter, "The Aztec Dog."
> The song "Wind Beneath My Wings" was also recorded under the title "Hero."
> "And Still I Rise" is an excellent poem by Maya Angelou.

❧ EXERCISE 15.5 ❧

Insert quotation marks where necessary in the following sentences.

1. If Damon continues at this pace, we can expect him to become a star athlete, said his coach.

2. We cannot, said Mr. Hord, afford to pay these people.

3. The envelope was stamped Confidential.

4. The court reporter read, Yes, I am responsible for the error.

5. Don't blame me for what happened here, said Simone. I'm only an innocent bystander.

6. I read the article Living to Please Yourself.

7. Angelica's favorite song is Evergreen.

8. Denise said, That St. Pucci dress is gorgeous.

9. The trailing purple petunias, he said, look magnificent on the deck.

10. Danté exclaimed, The brisk wind howled and moved through the branches of the pine trees.

HYPHENS

- Hyphens are used to form various compound words. The hyphen indicates that the connected words are to be understood as a single grammatical element:

    My *brother-in-law* was appointed secretary of the organization. (compound noun)

    The *12-inch* ruler is a standard measuring instrument. (compound modifier)

    The second-, third-, and fourth-floor meeting rooms have not been cleaned today. (series of compound modifiers)

    This is an *up-to-date* book. (multiword adjective)

    Thirty-five dollars will cover the cost of the luncheon. (compound number)

- Most prefixes and suffixes are spelled without using hyphens, but a few (including *ex-*, *self-*, *quasi-*, and *-elect*) do require a hyphen:

    Lenore, my *ex-roommate*, has a lot of *self-confidence*.
    Mr. Johnson is *president-elect* of his alumni association.

- Hyphens can be used to indicate spelling letter by letter:

    The word *accommodate* is spelled *a-c-c-o-m-m-o-d-a-t-e*.

ॐ EXERCISE 15.6 ॐ

Insert hyphens where necessary in the following sentences.

1. What out of date clothes she wore to work today!
2. The 20 acre lot provides enough space to build a huge apartment building.
3. Will eighty five table settings suffice for the convention dinner?
4. Please fix the railings on the fifth, sixth, and seventh floor balconies.
5. Her sister in law has no luck when it comes to keeping a job.

DASHES

- Dashes may be used to set off parenthetical comments or elements, especially if they contain internal commas:

    Three years ago—at the insistence of my brother, my sister, and my aunt—I opened a day-care center.

- A dash may also indicate an abrupt break or change in thought:

    Let's purchase them—well, first I'd better make sure I have enough money! "Why you little—" the man shouted at the culprit.

✢ EXERCISE 15.7 ✢

Insert dashes where needed in the following sentences.

1. The teacher realizing that the student needed remediation, counseling, and financial assistance made every effort to help.
2. The newspaper, the radio, and the television all are reliable news sources.
3. The four pilots Rudy Scott, Malcolm Knox, Roger Chan, and Kent Ward attended the same training school.
4. The elite of the group assembled to make plans for the reception the others were not concerned.
5. The ballroom furniture tables and chairs have been refinished.
6. His only concern was his looks in other words, what he would wear on his date.
7. Someday mark my words you'll be sorry you didn't learn a trade.
8. "One's aim ought always to be to leave whatever one touches better than one found it" at least according to Benjamin Mays.
9. My favorite meal grilled salmon is on the menu today.
10. Her only human frailty or so she thinks is criticizing others.

APOSTROPHE

The apostrophe has three uses: to show possession, to show that letters of a word have been omitted (contraction), and to form the plural of abbreviations.

Possession

- To form the possessive of a singular noun, add 's:

    man's hat   Charles's hat   my boss's hat

- To form the possessive of a plural noun ending in s, add just the apostrophe:

    bosses' coats   refugees' coats   the Adamses' coats

- To form the possessive of a plural noun not ending in s, add 's:

    men's coats   children's books

- When two or more nouns have joint ownership, only the last noun shows possession; when the nouns represent individual ownership, each noun must show possession:

    Carlester and Eddie's contract with Textron will expire soon. (The two men have a single contract.)

    Carlester's and Eddie's contract with Textron will expire soon. (Each man has a contract.)

Contraction

- An apostrophe marks the spot where letters have been omitted in words that are written to reflect how they are spoken:

    cannot   can't
    Madam   Ma'am
    going   goin'

Plurals of Abbreviations

- You may use *'s* to indicate the plural of an abbreviation or other short word that might be confusing otherwise:

  all A's and B's

  earned two M.B.A.'s

- Most abbreviations and all acronyms are pluralized without using the apostrophe:

  nos.   VCRs

ᔯ EXERCISE 15.8 ᔰ

Correct all errors with apostrophes in the following sentences.

1. Conner got all As and Bs on his report card.
2. I wo'nt be needing these old CD's much longer.
3. The Jones dentist is a member of the American Dental Association.
4. Bettys pain subsided after she took some ibuprofen.
5. The childrens sandbox is filled to capacity with red river rocks.

PARENTHESES

- Parentheses are used to set off nonessential information:

  Please send me the report on Thursday (I don't like to transact business on Fridays), and I will reply the same day.

- Parentheses are used to enclose enumerators in lists:

  Please submit the following items: (1) Social Security card, (2) driver's license, and (3) birth certificate.

  This brochure explains (a) your pension plan, (b) your continuing education package, and (c) your insurance coverage.

- Parentheses can enclose appositives inserted to ensure clarity:

> An infinitive consists of the base (uninflected) form of the verb preceded by the marker *to*.
>
> The total cost will be three hundred thousand dollars ($300,000).

ᴥ *EXERCISE 15.9* ᴥ

Supply parentheses where necessary in the following sentences.

1. The term of the loan was thirty 30 days.
2. Follow these instructions carefully: 1 remove film, 2 cover with a paper towel, 3 place in the center of the microwave, and 4 microwave on high for 45 seconds.
3. The repairmen if you want to call them that couldn't repair my leaky faucet.
4. She's quitting her job tomorrow what a joke because she didn't receive a promotion.
5. A sentence must contain at least one main independent clause.

VIRGULE

- The *virgule*, also known as the *slash, slant, solidus,* or *diagonal*, is used to form fractions, certain abbreviations, and certain expressions such as *and/or* or *poet/mathematician* to show that the terms are interchangeable. In these uses, no space should be placed before or after the mark.

> Surprisingly, our taxes have decreased by *5/8* percent since we moved here.
> The parcel was sent Tuesday morning, *c/o* Gene Gaines.
> The drive will be spearheaded by Charles Hubbard *and/or* Velma Smith.

- In quotations of poetry, the virgule, with a space on each side, is used to show where each line of poetry ends:

> The children sang: "Humpty Dumpty sat on a wall. / Humpty Dumpty had a great fall. / All the king's horses and all the king's men / Couldn't put Humpty together again."

UNDERSCORE

- The underscore is used in handwritten and typewritten documents to emphasize words and to set off the titles of books, magazines, newspapers, record albums, television shows, and movies. In typeset or computer-generated documents, underscoring is converted to italic (slanted) type:

The word <u>ain't</u> should <u>never</u> be
   used in serious writing.

The title of the book is <u>Easy Living</u>.

Mrs. Dougherty bought a copy
   of <u>Worldwide</u> magazine.

Our newspaper, the <u>Courier-Times</u>,
   is delivered at 4 a.m. every day.

Michael Jackson's <u>Bad</u> album made
   him a star around the world.

We watch <u>Nightline</u> whenever we
   stay up late.

My niece saw <u>Shrek</u> five times!

The word *ain't* should *never* be
   used in serious writing.

The title of the book is *Easy Living.*

Mrs. Dougherty bought a copy
   of *Worldwide* magazine.

Our newspaper, the *Courier-Times,*
   is delivered at 4 a.m. every day.

Michael Jackson's *Bad* album made
   him a star around the world.

We watch *Nightline* whenever we
   stay up late.

My niece saw *Shrek* five times!

❧ EXERCISE 15.10 ❧

Insert virgules or underscores where they are needed in the following sentences.

1. Mark Delano stars in the television show Moonlight.
2. Mr. Wilkins always misuses the words except and accept.
3. The utility stock has decreased 1 2 percent this month.
4. Articles in the Patent Attorney newsletter are always interesting.
5. Please send me a copy of the book Moby Dick by Herman Melville.
6. You must purchase Dante's new album, Drastic Measures.
7. Tara's favorite rhyme starts out, "Three blind mice, Three blind mice, See how they run, See how they run."
8. The Scarlet Letter is a book that I read many years ago.
9. I season green beans with onions and or shallots.
10. In what year did Midnight Cowboy win the Oscar as best picture?

PERIOD

- A period marks the end of any sentence that is not a question or an exclamation:

  We left the ship five minutes after it docked. (declarative sentence)

  Don't touch that button. (imperative sentence or command)

  Fallon asked where the museum was located. (indirect quotation)

  Would you kindly reply within five days. (polite request)

- A period marks the end of an abbreviation:

  The package was sent *c.o.d.* to 501 Main *St.*, Topeka, *Kans.*, for delivery tomorrow.

  The registration period begins at 8:30 *a.m.*

  Jonathan *B.* Colby, *Ph.D.*

  Note: Use no periods with *acronyms,* such as IBM, NATO, and other abbreviations written using capital letters.

- A period serves as the decimal point, marking the barrier between whole numbers (to the left) and fractions (to the right):

  98.6 degrees

QUESTION MARK

- A question mark signals the end of a direct question:

  What impact do you think the merger will have on our benefits?

- In a series of questions, a question mark may be used after each alternative:

  Does the plane land at La Guardia Airport? Kennedy? Newark? Some other airport?

EXCLAMATION POINT

- Use an exclamation point after a word, clause, phrase, or sentence that expresses a high degree of emotion:

    Wow!   Ouch! That hurt!

❧ EXERCISE 15.11 ❧

Insert periods, question marks, or exclamation points where necessary in the following sentences. Capitalize where necessary.

1. I would ask what impelled them to separate, wouldn't you
2. Whew this office is stuffy
3. They delivered the package cod yesterday
4. What is the possibility of acquiring a federal loan A grant A fellowship
5. Gosh this is scary
6. His father put the treadmill in the attic because he wasn't using it
7. What a day
8. Who was responsible for the problems we experienced
9. I give up
10. I get on North Blvd where it intersects with Hillman Ave near the county line, right

Review Test
Chapters 11–15

A. *Mark C for correct sentences, and mark F for sentence fragments.*

_____ 1. Panoramic view of the city below.

_____ 2. Govern yourselves accordingly.

_____ 3. The inhabitants of Old Quebec City are French-speaking people.

_____ 4. Octagonal cocktail table with Queen Anne legs.

_____ 5. Masseuse skillfully massaged her legs and the nape of her neck.

_____ 6. Being as shrewd and calculating as ever.

_____ 7. To germinate for several days in direct sunlight.

_____ 8. Golden hues of yellow and orange blossoms in the well-manicured yard.

_____ 9. To paint a clear picture of the bordering town five miles from the edge of town.

_____ 10. But figured it was best to propose an alternative.

_____ 11. Shirley grew weary before she reached the top of the Acropolis in Greece.

_____ 12. Studied the ancient ruins of Babylon.

_____ 13. Being notified of the disturbing news.

_____ 14. Ramon examined the skeletal remains to satisfy the requirements of his class.

_____ 15. Scouting in unknown territory in the middle of nowhere.

B. *Mark C for correct sentences. Mark F for fused sentences, and mark CS for comma splices.*

_____ 1. She received acclaim for her cosmetology skills she won first prize in the 2004 hair stylist competition.

_____ 2. That Grecian urn is symbolic of the ancient Roman battles.

_____ 3. Robert displayed his collection of paintings and sculptures to encourage an interest in the perpetuation of the African-American culture.

_____ 4. Dr. Martin Luther King Jr. completed his undergraduate studies at Morehouse College, he is thought by many to be the greatest civil rights activist.

_____ 5. Elvis Presley contributed to the USS *Arizona* Memorial Fund he held a sold-out concert to raise the money.

_____ 6. Hawaiian Islands natives called Pearl Harbor the "Water of Pearl" a vast number of pearl oysters filled the harbor.

_____ 7. A massive rock garden containing rocks from the seven continents encircles the yard, an explosion of colorful flowers native to Hawaii is the center of attraction.

_____ 8. The city council decided to recommend the redesign of the house at the end of the street and declare it a landmark.

_____ 9. Many people have been healed as a result of using home remedies.

_____ 10. Vanity proved to be her downfall no one was surprised when they heard the news of her defeat.

_____ 11. We heard that the greatest comedy of all time is to be simulcast at 8 p.m.

_____ 12. To lose weight, Cecilia dieted and exercised, she also participated in an extensive weight-loss program.

_____ 13. The bloodhound received a diamond and sapphire necklace and a trophy for winning the American Kennel Club's K9 Advantix competition, its owner received a $50,000 check from the American Kennel Club and a $10,000 IAMS Viewers Choice check payable to the parent breed club.

_____ 14. Two attorneys represented the man accused of making counterfeit money in a nearby barn.

_____ 15. David's face twitched uncontrollably under the extreme pressure of the intensive interrogation.

C. Write DM for dangling modifier and MM for misplaced modifier. Write C for the one correct sentence.

_____ 1. Kenneth saw a spider in his shoe putting on his pants.

_____ 2. Stroking mightily, the shore was reached.

_____ 3. Run over by a car, I saw a deer.

_____ 4. Paul caught a glimpse of the huge catfish as it fell from his hook.

_____ 5. I suddenly headed for the ocean in my jeep which was fifty miles away.

D. Change each incorrect group to the correct parallel form. Write the correct answer in the blank to the right. Write OK if the words in the group are parallel. Four word groups are correct.

_____ 1. inside the stadium, near the coliseum, the giant white wall

_____ 2. talking in riddles, singing in bass, walked in long strides

_____ 3. flute player, organist, pianist

_____ 4. year-end summary, earth-shattering question, two-lane highway

_____ 5. technically, economically, physically

_____ 6. bonding, tacking, securing

_____ 7. subway, freeway, passage

_____ 8. small-town saga, three-way lane, triple-decker sandwich

_____ 9. to consider, decide, to determine

_____ 10. to dance, prancing, glancing

E. Punctuate the following sentences using commas and semicolons.

1. The bank is unable to give you a loan you don't have any tangible assets.
2. Our homeowners insurance offers protection from fire and natural disasters it offers no mold coverage.
3. My co-worker is African American my pastor is Hispanic and my cousin is Anglo Saxon.
4. Put the Oriental vase the crystal glasses and the antique china in the cabinet.
5. My first daughter, Marie, is nine my second daughter, Peggy, is five and my son, Dexter, is one.
6. All entrants must be witty fun-loving individuals with pleasing personalities.
7. Rickety knees are a family characteristic high cholesterol is also.
8. Graduation is set for May 15 2005.
9. The movie a great comedy will air two weeks from today.
10. Alexander said "The fraternity must comply with the university rules."
11. I can if given the opportunity succeed in my career of choice.
12. Henry enjoys exhilarating motorcycle rides breathtaking helicopter rides and life-threatening hiking excursions.
13. As agreed customers must pay parking fees before 5 p.m. weekdays.
14. The architectural style of the buildings at San Marco in Italy the Louvre Museum in France and the ruins of the Acropolis in Greece are astounding.
15. Discrepancies are directly related to irresponsible employees within the department layoffs are imminent.

F. Place colons, quotation marks, hyphens, dashes, and apostrophes where necessary.

1. James digestive system is out of whack.
2. You should on second thought consider the possibility of leasing a larger vehicle.
3. The Jones 18-wheeler truck was repossessed because they failed to make timely payments.

4. The mens line of clothing is more popular than the womens line at this particular store.

5. My brother in law swindled his brothers and sisters out of a fortune.

6. She spelled her name a s h l e e.

7. My ex professor lectured nonstop with much zeal and enthusiasm.

8. The following items are needed for the picnic on Saturday pickles, mustard, and buns.

9. The two page articles reprinted in May, September, and December proved to be very popular.

10. The literary reference should be written Worthword Altrusa Books, 2005.

11. *How to Lose Weight in Two Days A Practical Workbook* arrived at the bookstore yesterday.

12. There is, said Mr. Ramsey, something strange about that young man sitting in the corner.

13. Dominque replied, It was not my intention to cause dissension among the members of the committee.

14. The supervisor demanded a day by day account of the inventory.

15. There is a possibility that I will delete some of the assignments, said the professor.

G. *Punctuate the following sentences using parentheses, diagonals, underscores, periods, question marks, and exclamation points.*

1. When you travel outside the county, be sure to take the following items: 1 a passport, 2 an ATM card, and 3 some cash.

2. John's retirement check was sent co Mrs. Effie Smith.

3. The personal trainer distributed a copy of The Young and Fit magazine to all of the young women in the group.

4. Do you think it's just a figment of his imagination

5. It was decided that 1 4 of the funds would be donated to the alumni association.

6. In all honesty, what is your opinion of the decision to hire a secretary with no computer experience

7. One of the best novels of all time is The Scarlet Letter.

8. Wow That news spread like wild fire.

9. Does she have a PhD in English or math?

10. By the end of the day, the temperature was 1006 degrees Fahrenheit.

~ *16* ~

Numbers

GENERAL RULES

- The numbers *zero* through *nine* are usually written in words; figures are used for numbers 10 and above:

    Donald speaks four languages.
    Margarite has 15 pairs of shoes.

- A number that begins a sentence must be written in words. However, if the number cannot be written using one or two words, add words or rearrange the sentence so that the number does not come first, and write the number in figures:

    Fifty-three people witnessed the terrible explosion.
    A total of 553 people witnessed the terrible explosion.

- Approximations above nine that can be expressed in one or two words may be written in either figures or numbers. However, figures are more emphatic and conform to the rule for the use of general numbers.

    Around 500 people went to the rock concert in Trenton.
    Approximately seventy-five students crammed the hallway.

- In standard American usage, four-digit numbers may be written with or without an internal comma:

    4,000 years ago   *or*   4000 years ago

    Four-digit dates and page numbers do not have a comma:

    the year 1989   turn to page 1120

    Longer numbers always take a comma to separate each group of three digits from right to left:

    10,000 years ago   a population of 30,825,991

- In metric measurements, a space replaces the comma:

    4 000 liters   *or*   4000 liters   10 000 kilometers

- Model, serial, and other code numbers are written in figures without symbols or punctuation:

    Our old Model 3 refrigerator was replaced with a new Model 5.

    Your computer, serial no. F38383888, was shipped to you yesterday, waybill A255159Z.

- Certain other numbers have traditional formats:

    Telephone number: (102) 304-0506

    Social Security number: 987-65-4321

    ZIP code: 90210-0210

- Round numbers in the millions and higher are expressed using a combination of figures and words. If one million is used as an approximation, it is usually written out; otherwise, it is written 1 million. Decimals with *million, billion,* and so on should not go beyond one decimal place.

> Someone won $5.2 million in the lottery last evening.
> We hope to sell one million copies of the new album.
> Sales topped 1 million cars over the past three years.

- The plural of a figure is formed by adding *s* with no apostrophe:

> Several 7s appeared on the computer screen.
> The 1850s was a time of great literary writing.

✐ EXERCISE 16.1 ✐

Correct all errors with numbers in the following sentences. If a sentence contains no errors, write **OK** *in the blank.*

_____ 1. This quaint cottage is approximately one hundred years old.
_____ 2. About 400 people attended the auction last night.
_____ 3. Five hundred seventy-three entries came in overnight.
_____ 4. Approximately 1 million copies of the book were distributed nationwide.
_____ 5. 83 foreign-exchange students arrived on American Airlines flight 1143.
_____ 6. The merger cost the corporation $4 million.
_____ 7. The king-size bed accommodates three pillow shams.
_____ 8. We cited twelve instances of unfair treatment.
_____ 9. Gordon asked for all the fives in the deck.
_____ 10. The company's losses totaled $11,535 million last year.

WEIGHTS AND MEASURES

- Exact weights and measures are expressed using figures:

    This bowl holds 4 gallons of punch.
    We had to walk 2½ miles to school.

- A single measurement expressed in more than one unit is written without commas:

    Ella weighed 6 pounds 7 ounces when she was born.
    The hallway is 7 feet 3 inches long.

  Note that except in scientific or statistical contexts, the units of measurement should not be abbreviated.

- Page numbers are written in figures, and the word *page* is not capitalized:

    The article continues on page 23.

- Two consecutive numbers that act as adjectives modifying the same noun are not separated by a comma. The shorter or simpler number should be written in words.

    I bought a sheet of twenty 37-cent stamps.
    The artist painted thirty 6-by-8-inch acrylics for the exhibition.

- When two independent figures appear consecutively in a sentence, the figures may be separated with commas, but it is better to revise the sentence to separate them:

    Acceptable: In 1998, 30 students participated in the marathon.
    Better: In 1998, a total of 30 students participated in the marathon.
    Better: Thirty students participated in the marathon in 1998.

❧ EXERCISE 16.2 ❧

Correct all errors with numbers in the following sentences.

1. Turn to page ninety-three for additional information on carnivorous animals.
2. My podiatrist gave me a prescription for 20 200-milligram Vicoprofen pain capsules.
3. Can you determine the 5 spices used in preparing this delicious casserole?
4. That box weighed two pounds three ounces before Jan's clothes were packed in it.
5. Our club donated nine booklets of thirty-seven-cent stamps.

❧ EXERCISE 16.3 ❧

*Correct all errors with numbers in the following sentences. If a sentence contains no errors, write **OK** in the blank.*

_____ 1. Brother Edwards's famous pancake recipe requires two cups of flour.
_____ 2. Mother shelled five bushels of peas and put them in the freezer.
_____ 3. Her zealous fan had 2 dozen roses delivered to her dressing room.
_____ 4. I need thirty yards of silk fabric to make my bedroom draperies.
_____ 5. The caterer ordered 10 gallons of punch for the wedding reception.
_____ 6. A gallon of juice weighs four pounds.
_____ 7. This entire package contains only 5 grams of fat.
_____ 8. The water boy gave each player two 500-milliliter sports drinks.
_____ 9. How many acres is 30 000 square meters?
_____ 10. Pierre poured two tablespoons of flavoring into the mixing bowl.

RELATED NUMBERS

- Numbers used similarly in the same context should be expressed in the same form. For example, if figures are used for any numbers in a discussion, they should be used for all related numbers in that discussion:

  Aisha has 110 old pennies and 8 old dimes.

  The contractor built 220 condominiums, 68 single-family homes, and 2 apartment complexes.

  The newspaper's circulation of just over 1,000,000 surges to 3,893,939 copies on Sundays.

- Unrelated numbers used in the same sentence are considered individually in determining whether they should be expressed in figures or words:

  Last year, we bought three vehicles to transport our eight employees and 22 head of cattle.

ꓜ EXERCISE 16.4 ꓜ

*Correct all errors with numbers in the following sentences. If a sentence contains no errors, write **OK** in the blank.*

_____ 1. My talented friend wrote 12 books, opened 4 businesses, and received three academic degrees in a period of nine years.

_____ 2. Our company generated 2,112,189 pieces of correspondence this year and 969,000 last year.

_____ 3. SunView, Inc., built 544 decks and 6 patios in a month.

_____ 4. The little girl grasped 12 quarters, three dimes, and 11 pennies in the palm of her hand.

_____ 5. Mary's goal is to open two boutiques within five years.

MONEY

- Amounts of money are expressed in figures. Omit the decimals and zeros in expressing whole-dollar amounts, even when they are used with mixed-dollar amounts.

  Her jacket cost $659.95.

  The prices of the items were $299, $45.63, $5, and $73.43.

- Write out the word *cents* for amounts under $1 unless they appear in conjunction with related amounts of money of $1 or more.

  I remember when first-class stamps cost 5 cents.

  I bought items that cost $54, $8.45, and $0.73.

- Round amounts of money in the millions and higher follow the rules for other large numbers. Use a dollar sign before the figure.

  The studio cost $13.5 million.

  It will cost $7,500,000 to renovate the Hanson Mansion and $1,543,000 to renovate the Pearson Mansion.

DECIMALS AND PERCENTAGES

- Numbers containing decimals are expressed in figures. Place a zero before a decimal that expresses an amount less than unity (1).

  Each question was given a weight of 3.3 points.

  Spring water is sold in 0.5-liter bottles.

- Write percentages in figures followed by the word *percent*. The percent symbol (%) is used only in statistical or technical tables or forms.

  Her line of credit was based on 10 percent of her yearly income.

  We anticipate a 0.9 percent increase in sales this year.

FRACTIONS

- Simple fractions that can be expressed in two words are written in word form and are hyphenated.

    She ate two-thirds of her cheesecake and gave the rest to me.

    It takes a two-thirds majority vote to ratify the contract.

- Figures are used to express long and awkward fractions, fractions used for technical purposes, and fractions combined with whole numbers.

    The newly discovered moon is only 1/250 the size of our moon.

    We walked 2½ miles to the nearest service station.

    The lumber company did not have ⅛-inch screws.

❧ EXERCISE 16.5 ❧

*Correct all errors with numbers in the following sentences. If a sentence contains no errors, write **OK** in the blank.*

_____ 1. Stanley paid one thousand dollars for my beautiful, brown leather jacket.

_____ 2. The camping equipment cost $89.95, $30, $23.99, and $5.00, respectively.

_____ 3. A small bar of candy is priced at fifty-five cents.

_____ 4. We paid $46,000 for our first home and $1,112,000 for our second home.

_____ 5. The homeowner personally designed 40 percent of the house plan.

_____ 6. The average weight of a $2.99 seedless watermelon is 15.6 pounds, which works out to about nineteen cents a pound.

_____ 7. Your monthly credit card payment is based on 12% of your total account balance.

_____ 8. Roderick has finished reading about 3/4 of the book.

_____ 9. The knobs are attached to the drawers with one-fourth-inch screws.

_____ 10. We ran two and a half miles to the park.

DATES

- When month and day appear together, use cardinal numbers (1, 2, 3, etc.) for the date. When expressing days without the month or that stand alone, use ordinal numbers (first, 10th, 31st, etc.).

> My foot surgery is scheduled for May 31, 2004.
> The March 12 payment is 60 days late.
> My mortgage payment is due on the 15th of each month.

- When only month and year are mentioned, the year may be set off with commas or not, as long as the format is consistent throughout the document (see Chapter 15):

> the May, 2004, issue   *or*   the May 2004 issue

- Note that a year with four digits never takes a comma.

CLOCK TIME

- To express clock time, figures are used with *a.m.*, *p.m.*, *noon*, or *midnight*. Omit the colon and zeros with even times, even if they appear in conjunction with times expressed in hours and minutes. *Noon* and *midnight* may be used with or without the figure 12. When these terms are used with other clock times containing *a.m.* or *p.m.*, include the figure 12. Never use *a.m.* or *p.m.* following *noon* or *midnight*.

> Her aunt arrived at the airport at 11:47 a.m.
> Her flight left at 9:43 a.m. and arrived at 12 noon.
> The package must be post marked before midnight Thursday.

- Either words or figures may be used with *o'clock:*

> The class is scheduled to meet at nine o'clock.
> The class is scheduled to meet at 9 o'clock.

- Phrases such as "in the morning," "in the afternoon," and "at night" may follow clock times expressed with *o'clock* but not with *a.m.* or *p.m.*:

> I will practice my piano lesson at 11 o'clock in the morning.
>
> Come to the gym at three o'clock in the afternoon.
>
> Start watching the movie at 8 o'clock at night.

- Use words when even clock hours of the day are expressed without *a.m.*, *p.m.*, or *o'clock*. When both hours and minutes are expressed, use either words or figures.

> The choir will sing at eight tonight.
>
> Our little puppy has been missing since 7:30.
>
> Our little puppy has been missing since seven-thirty.

PERIODS OF TIME

- Periods of time that can be expressed in one or two words are usually written in word form when they are used in a general way. Periods of time that cannot be expressed in one or two words should be written in figure form.

  General references to time expressed in hours, minutes, or seconds are treated as general numbers: the numbers nine and below are written out, and figures are used for 10 and up.

> Latasha's term paper must be submitted in ten days.
>
> You have one week to frame Dean Leuva's house.
>
> The insurance policy will expire at the end of 12 months.
>
> It takes at least two years to write a good book.
>
> You have exactly 48 hours to vacate the premises.
>
> It takes six hours to view the tape.

- Time period data in financial or business contexts are expressed in figures:

> The certificate of deposit matures in 90 days.
>
> You have qualified for a 15-year mortgage at 5.75 percent with 2 points payable at closing.

*Correct all errors with numbers in the following sentences. If a sentence contains no errors, write **OK** in the blank.*

_____ 1. You will receive a refund in 3 to 5 days.

_____ 2. Expected pay dates are the 15th and 30 of the month.

_____ 3. Your rental contract will renew on the 31st.

_____ 4. The Benson Alumni Association luncheon begins at noon p.m.

_____ 5. I expect you to finish the wall papering in 2 days.

_____ 6. The play *Wait until Dark* premieres at 8 p.m. tomorrow.

_____ 7. The statute of limitations expires in twelve days.

_____ 8. You have seventy-two hours to back out of the contract.

_____ 9. The winner's savings bond matures in five years.

_____ 10. This policy expires at one minute before midnight on June 30, 2006.

AGES AND ANNIVERSARIES

- Ages and anniversaries that can be expressed in one or two words are generally written in word form. If they require more than two words, they are written in figures. Figures are also used when an age appears as an appositive after a person's name. Figures are used in a legal or technical sense. Figures are also used to express exact terms of years, months, and days.

  I turn thirty-four in July.

  The city celebrated its 120th anniversary in 1999.

  The engineer, 30, is quickly climbing the corporate ladder.

  You will be unable to drive until you reach age 16.

  I am 53 years, 9 months, and 27 days old.

ADDRESSES

- House numbers are expressed in figures except for the house number 1:

    David lives at One Main Street.

    I reside at 37 Madron Avenue.

- Street names that are numbered nine or below are expressed in word form with ordinal numbers. Street names numbered above nine are written in figures, with the street name in ordinal form (i.e., using -*th*, -*nd*, -*rd*, and -*st* endings).

    One of the finest boutiques in town is located on Sixth Avenue.

    The John twins reside at 3333 22nd Street.

    The architect moved to 3233 East 42nd Place.

- Apartment numbers, box numbers, suite numbers, and route numbers are expressed in figures:

    2833 Prosper Drive, Apt. 15

    P.O. Box 12

    Jansen Medical Center, Suite 1121

    Route 53

ORDINALS

- Ordinal numbers (*first, second, third,* etc.) that can be written in one or two words are generally expressed in word form except as noted elsewhere in this chapter:

    This is the thirty-fifth reunion of the Class of 1967.

EXERCISE 16.7

Correct all errors with numbers in the following sentences. If a sentence contains no errors, write **OK** in the blank.

_____ 1. Mother was 32 when I was born.

_____ 2. My brother is thirty-nine years eleven months and twenty-two days old.

_____ 3. This is the 11th anniversary of the Mason Scholarship Awards Banquet.

_____ 4. Bancroft Mansion is located at 1 Pinson Street in the center of downtown.

_____ 5. Jean received a diamond watch on her twentieth wedding anniversary.

_____ 6. Many antique shops that once lined 7th Avenue have gone out of business.

_____ 7. Which architect designed the house at 2114 West Thirty-Third Street?

_____ 8. All of the houses on West Seventh Street were demolished to accommodate a rejuvenation project by the city.

_____ 9. Architect Frank Lloyd Wright drew the blueprints for the old mansion on South Twenty-Second Street in Washington, D.C.

_____ 10. Tuesday commemorates the 20th anniversary of the scholarship foundation.

EXERCISE 16.8

Correct all errors with numbers in the following sentences. If a sentence contains no errors, write **OK** in the blank.

_____ 1. The two firms merged 18 years ago.

_____ 2. 8 men and 2 women rode in the stretch limousine.

_____ 3. In 1972, 523 new houses were built by Peterson & Jackson Builders.

_____ 4. The publishing company sold seven hundred seventy-five copies of my book.

_____ 5. My new air-conditioning unit will be installed on April twenty-third.

_____ 6. The book contains sixty-six chapters.

_____ 7. 28,382,000 e-mail messages were sent to the company last month.

_____ 8. Harold Bowman's address is 5432 South 2nd Street.

_____ 9. She presented her report in 3 parts, 2 of which contained statistical data.

_____ 10. Her paper consisted of three hundred ninety-three words, of which one hundred ninety-four were 1-syllable words and sixty-five were 3-syllable words.

EXERCISE 16.9

Correct all errors with numbers in the following sentences. If a sentence contains no errors, write **OK** *in the blank.*

_____ **1.** Our inquiry of the 14th of August must have crossed your reply.

_____ **2.** In my letter dated 14 April, I addressed 2 of your concerns raised in your letter dated 8 May.

_____ **3.** That store carries over three hundred twenty-five items priced at twenty-five cents.

_____ **4.** The report is 78 pages long and includes 35 illustrations.

_____ **5.** Thirteen computers, eight desks, and seven chairs are missing from the inventory.

_____ **6.** Their office has relocated from Seven McMillan Street to 2344 West Thirty-Fifth Street.

_____ **7.** The librarian ordered eight copies of *Texas* and thirteen copies of *Hawaii*.

_____ **8.** 14 professors were hired last year, bringing the total faculty count to 122.

_____ **9.** I mailed 263 pages to the publishing company today.

_____ **10.** Our enrollment will probably exceed twelve thousand this semester.

EXERCISE 16.10

In the following sentences, some of the numbers are written correctly and some are not. Place an **X** *in the column headed "Right" if all the numbers in a sentence are written correctly. Place an* **X** *in the column headed "Wrong" if there are errors in the sentence. Underscore the errors.*

	Right	Wrong
1. The cost of living rose one-half of 1 percent.	_____	_____
2. We will meet at 3 p.m. sharp.	_____	_____
3. Henry was given a $3.00 raise last week.	_____	_____

	Right	Wrong
4. Your refund is $.35.	_____	_____
5. Three hundred new positions were created.	_____	_____
6. I received a thirty percent discount on the picture.	_____	_____
7. Your doctor's appointment is scheduled for Wednesday, May 9.	_____	_____
8. Darlene lives at 105 East 33rd Street.	_____	_____
9. Please turn to page seven of your textbook.	_____	_____
10. The chaise lounge measured 78 by 28 inches.	_____	_____

ᔥ *EXERCISE 16.11* ᔣ

Correct all errors with numbers in the following sentences. If a sentence contains no errors, write **OK** *in the blank.*

_____ 1. The books are packed in a box that measures 25 by 22 by 10½ inches.

_____ 2. Louise's answer was 0.1334, while Jade's answer was 0.1333.

_____ 3. The engineers meticulously designed the one-eighth-inch mechanical part.

_____ 4. The health center is exactly twelve and one-half miles from my house.

_____ 5. The vote was one hundred twenty to nine in favor of the new policy.

❧ 17 ❧

Capitalization

BEGINNING WORDS

- Capitalize the first words of sentences, quoted sentences, lines of poetry, independent phrases, and items in an outline:

    Your last comment was unnecessary.

    He implored, "Tell me the secret to getting a promotion."

    1. Items needed for camping
    - **a.** Tent
    - **b.** Flashlight
    - **c.** Canteen
    - **d.** Insect repellent

- Generally, the first word following a colon is not capitalized. However, capitalize the first word when the material following the colon (1) begins with a proper noun, (2) consists of two or more sentences, (3) presents a formal rule, (4) begins a vertical listing, or (5) requires emphasis.

    The teacher requested the following: drawing paper, pens, pencils, and a drawing board.

    We will tour three places in the eastern Mediterranean: Malta, Italy, and Turkey.

    Here are the three questions she asked: Do you really want to attend a technical school? Will the courses transfer to a university? How long will it take for you to complete your degree requirements?

Please submit the following:

1. Your 2002 income tax statement
2. Your last paycheck stub
3. Your last utility bill

PROPER NAMES AND ADJECTIVES

· Proper nouns (names of persons, places, and unique things) and adjectives derived from proper nouns are capitalized:

I live in the Sunrise District of Houston, Texas.
The benefit was held at the Mason Wright Center on Anderson Avenue South.
The Golden Gate Bridge spans the entrance to San Francisco Bay.
The first mall in our neighborhood was the Parks Center Mall.
I love Swiss cheese.

· Capitalize brand names and trade names. Words that describe the type or kind of product (such as vacuum cleaner, computer, television) are not capitalized unless they are coined derivatives that are considered part of the trade name.

This is a General Electric freezer.
There is a Dell computer in the library.
We bought a new Vac-U-Matic.

ᔓ EXERCISE 17.1 ᔐ

*Circle each capitalization error in the following sentences or lines. If an item has no errors, write **OK** in the blank.*

_____ 1. Elizabeth exclaimed, "you don't know how it feels to be criticized."
_____ 2. ramona captured his attention when she revealed her identity.

_____ **3.** The Wilsons bought property in the mountain meadows subdivision.

_____ **4.** This maytag washer will last a lifetime.

_____ **5.** Lucas said, "mark, never judge a man by his worldly possessions."

_____ **6.** Answer the following questions: Are you a Texas resident? Do you have a driver's license? Are you employed?

_____ **7.** My 5-ton trane air-conditioning and heating unit does not sufficiently cool or heat my 3,500-square-foot house.

_____ **8.** Kendra said, "the white orchids enhance Rena's sophisticated table setting."

_____ **9.** cecilia said, "I have a nostalgic feeling whenever I visit this library."

_____ **10.** Our amana refrigerator is equipped with food storage containers.

ABBREVIATIONS AND ACRONYMS

- Most abbreviations are capitalized only if the words they represent are capitalized. The exceptions to this rule are the abbreviations of academic degrees. Abbreviations usually end with a period.

  Please read pp. 502–647 in vol. 1 by Sept. 27.

  Go down Broad St. and turn right onto Grand Blvd.

  The professor will receive his M.S. degree in May.

- Acronyms are always capitalized and take no end punctuation:

  We work out at the YMCA.

  SIDS has claimed many a young life.

  My cousin is a CPA.

NUMBERED OR LETTERED ITEMS

- Nouns followed by numerals or letters are capitalized except in the case of page, paragraph, line, size, and verse references. The word _number,_ when needed, is abbreviated _no._ unless it appears at the beginning of a sentence.

The cafeteria issued Invoice 137603 for the banquet menu.

The microwave is Model 31B.

Turn to page 5, paragraph 2, line 4.

The government will issue Policy No. 8373 next week.

Number 8 is incorrectly stated.

PERSONAL TITLES

- Courtesy titles (*Miss., Mrs., Ms., Mr.*) are not commonly used when the full name is provided. However, if a woman is married, her married title (*Mrs.*) may be used. *Dr.* and *Professor* are used when they are used before a person's name.

    Capitalize a title representing a person's profession, company position, military rank, service rank, religious station, or political office only when it directly precedes the person's name. The same rule applies to titles indicating family relationship or nobility.

    When a person's title is used in place of his or her name, the title is usually not capitalized. However, in case of direct address, capitalize the title if it replaces the name.

    Donald Decou is a close friend of mine.

    Dr. Weatherspoon performed open-heart surgery on my uncle.

    I have heard that Professor Meltzer is an excellent teacher.

    She is professor of marketing at the university.

    May I submit my term paper next week, Professor?

    The policy was written by Colonel Johnson.

    Did you say that Senator Royce West is an African American?

    I'd like you to meet President Vernon Masters of the United Charities organization.

    Vernon Masters, president of the United Charities, is a highly influential person.

    My mother's sister, Aunt Nadia, is like a second mother to me.

    Is Prince Charles very popular?

- A person's title is always capitalized in business correspondence when it appears in the inside address, in the signature line, or on the envelope.

Dr. Jim Crimson, Director of Special Services

123 Marks Street

Agawam, MA 01001

Dear Dr. Crimson:

- When the title of an executive officer is used in an organization's formal rules, minutes, or bylaws, it is capitalized. Capitalize the title of a high-ranking government official when it is used in a formal context (an acknowledgment or introduction).

  > The Financial Secretary's report was thorough.
  >
  > Our President is also our hardest worker.

- Terms such as *ex-*, *-elect*, *late*, and *former* are not capitalized when they are combined with a title:

  > Since ex-President Holden was returned to office, our financial condition has worsened.
  >
  > President-elect Marcus Brennan appeared on television last night.
  >
  > The late President Eisenhower was a hero of the Second World War.
  >
  > All confidential papers were sent to former President Bill Clinton.

LITERARY AND ARTISTIC WORKS

- Capitalize the main words in the titles of all published works, including magazines, newspapers, books, albums, television shows, movies, and works of art. Do not capitalize articles, prepositions, or conjunctions unless they are the first or last word in the title. The titles of lengthy and freestanding works are italicized. (Underscore if italics are unavailable; see Chapter 15.)

  > Jim Olson's new magazine is titled *The Best of Texas*.
  >
  > Our local newspaper is the *Star-Telegram*.
  >
  > Have you read the novel *Texas* by James Michener?
  >
  > *The Eminem Show* was a top-selling CD in 2002.
  >
  > Mr. Pereira likes the television show *Fair Deal*.

We saw the movie *Men of Honor* on HBO last night.

The sculpture known as *Winged Victory* is as breathtaking as ever.

That famous portrait of James Whistler's mother is actually titled *Arrangement in Gray and Black, No. 1.*

- The titles of shorter works (such as poems and songs) and parts of longer works (such as essays, articles, chapters, and stories) are capitalized like other titles but are placed in quotation marks rather than italicized.

The hit song "My Heart Will Go On" is the theme from the movie *Titanic.*

Ali Madrid wrote the short story "Companions" in one week.

I read a wonderful essay titled "The Quiet Storm."

Dorothy found the article "Stress in a Changing Society" in *Health* magazine.

Turn to Chapter 3, "Fixing Leaky Faucets."

My favorite episode of *The Twilight Zone* is titled "To Serve Man."

✢ EXERCISE 17.2 ✢

Circle each capitalization error in the following sentences. If a sentence has no errors, write **OK** *in the blank.*

_____ 1. She earned a ph.d. in English.

_____ 2. What is the invoice number on the contractual agreement?

_____ 3. Proofreader's marks appear in paragraph 5, lines 10 and 11.

_____ 4. The position of vice president of operations no longer exists.

_____ 5. My favorite relative, uncle Jed, lives on a farm in Topeka, Kansas.

_____ 6. Many elegant gowns were designed for princess Diana.

_____ 7. Did you attend Louisiana State University, professor?

_____ 8. I wonder if Former Vice President Gore still craves the limelight.

_____ 9. The Late Secretary of State John Hawkins is buried in this cemetery.

_____ 10. Did you see *beauty and the beast* when you were in New York?

ACADEMIC SUBJECTS, COURSES, AND DEGREES

- The names of numbered courses and specific course titles are capitalized. However, in the names of academic subject areas, only proper nouns are capitalized.

  History 101

  Comparative Literature of the Eighteenth Century

  I took a history class in summer school.

  Maria was the most fluent speaker in her Spanish class.

- The names of academic degrees are usually not capitalized; however, the abbreviations for them, when used in conjunction with the name of an individual, do take capital letters:

  Darcus has a bachelor of science degree.

  Margaret Wang, Ed.D., M.S.W., will be our guest speaker.

  "Respectfully submitted, Ricardo Guzmán, Ph.D."

GROUPS, DATES, AND PLACES

- The main words in the names of organizations are capitalized:

  Black River Chamber of Commerce

  Fannie M. Heath Cultural Club

  Leukemia Foundation of the Americas

- The official names of departments, divisions, and offices in a business organization are capitalized. However, whenever a department or division name is referred to by its function because the official or specific name is unknown, do not capitalize.

He is taking classes in the Department of Sociology.

Are you still in the Business and Social Science Division?

The new professor in the history department has high expectations.

The board of directors met yesterday.

- Capitalize the names of bureaus, offices, divisions, departments, and agencies in government organizations:

The president supports the decisions of the Department of Defense officials.

You may obtain a copy of your birth certificate from the Bureau of Vital Statistics.

The proposal for the repair of Prosper Street was sent to the Division of Roads and Bridges.

⟩ EXERCISE 17.3 ⟨

*Circle each capitalization error in the following sentences. If a sentence has no errors, write **OK** in the blank.*

_____ 1. He wrote the chapter titled "carnivorous animals."

_____ 2. British literature II is not a prerequisite for obtaining an English degree.

_____ 3. Marilyn Ebbs, PH.D., resigned from her teaching position and accepted a job in administration.

_____ 4. Do you plan to take history during the second summer session?

_____ 5. Our club always donates to the American Cancer Society.

_____ 6. Report to the department of Human Resources if you are in need of financial assistance.

_____ 7. Carla attended the national education association convention in St. Louis.

_____ 8. Is american literature 201 a prerequisite for a degree in math?

_____ 9. Read the article titled "living on pennies."

_____ 10. Acquiring an ed.d. in administration requires stamina and perseverance.

GEOGRAPHICAL LOCATION

- The official or traditional names of places (mountains, valleys, oceans, lakes, parks, canals, harbors, bays, rivers, seas, islands, streets, cities, states, continents, and countries) are capitalized. Other geographical terms are not.

> Mount Everest is one of the most famous mountains in the world.
>
> Peaks Valley is located in California.
>
> The ship capsized in the Pacific Ocean.
>
> Lake Ontario is one of the five Great Lakes.
>
> Yellowstone National Park is located in northwestern Wyoming.
>
> The class learned about the Panama Canal in social studies.
>
> We dined at the exclusive restaurant on the dock of Main Street Harbor.
>
> Chesapeake Bay is an inlet of the Atlantic in Maryland and Virginia.
>
> The Canton River runs north and south of the city.
>
> Have you any knowledge of the Red Sea?
>
> Typhoon Lagoon is located on Disney property.
>
> I reside at 2312 Marks Place.
>
> My daughter lives in Bristow, Virginia.
>
> I know that Antarctica is one of the seven continents.
>
> The United States of America is a powerful, resourceful country.
>
> Our Mediterranean cruise includes a tour of the city of Venice.

- Capitalize the nicknames of geographical locations and conventional designations of neighborhoods and regions:

> New York City is known affectionately as the Big Apple.
>
> My father grew up on the South Side.
>
> We moved from the Upper Peninsula of Michigan to the West Coast.

- Points of the compass and their derivatives are capitalized in traditional designations for specific regions. They are not capitalized when they indicate direction or general location.

> Many movie studios are headquartered in Southern California.
>
> Have you seen the farmlands of the Midwest?

Henri lives in northern New Jersey but plans to move to west-central Florida when he retires.

Go west until you cross into eastern Kentucky.

DATES, TIME, TIME PERIODS, AND EVENTS

- Capitalize days of the week, months of the year, holidays, specific special events, and historical events or periods. The names of seasons, decades, and centuries are generally not capitalized. However, when a season is combined with a year, capitalize the season.

  The Curtisville Cultural Club meets on the first Tuesday of the month from October through June.

  We always have a barbecue on the Fourth of July.

  Lawrence and Erma hosted a beautiful Silver Anniversary reception a few years ago.

  My grandparents suffered in the Great Depression of the 1930s.

  I ordered a CD of classic songs of the fifties, sixties, and seventies.

  The twentieth century brought many new inventions.

  We started dating in Spring 2001.

ETHNIC AND RELIGIOUS REFERENCES

- References to a particular language, race, or culture are capitalized. Generic terms such as *black* and *white* when used in reference to race are usually not capitalized.

  ESL students must learn the principles and rules of the English language.

  Many Westerners fail to realize that the designation "Asian American" encompasses dozens of ethnic backgrounds.

  The Kwanzaa holiday is now celebrated by many African Americans.

  Cinco de Mayo commemorates a Mexican victory over French forces on May 5, 1862.

  Our new Venezuelan neighbor speaks Portuguese as well as Spanish.

217

- Capitalize references to specific religious groups:

   There are 50 million Catholics and more than 30 million Baptists in the United States.

CELESTIAL BODIES

- Capitalize the names of celestial bodies (constellations, asteroids, planets and their satellites, and stars). However, do not capitalize the terms *sun, moon,* and *earth* unless they are used as the names of specific bodies in the solar system.

   We live in a galaxy known as the Milky Way.

   Great bursts of radio waves emanated from the belt of Orion the Hunter.

   The most fascinating of Jupiter's many moons is Io.

   The Sun is 93 million miles from Earth.

   The sun shines on my kitchen window in the morning and warms the earth in the window box.

⅋ EXERCISE 17.4 ⅌

Circle each capitalization error in the following sentences. If a sentence has no errors, write **OK** *in the blank.*

_____ **1.** Is central park located in New York or Chicago?

_____ **2.** The Sanchez family moved to Houston, texas, from the rural southwest.

_____ **3.** Chicago is known as the windy city.

_____ **4.** Colonel Franklin lives in west Virginia.

_____ **5.** We will move north when we retire.

_____ **6.** Our office is closed Wednesdays and Fridays throughout the summer.

_____ **7.** The Fourteenth of July is a major holiday for the french.

_____ **8.** Tell me everything you know about the revolutionary war.

_____ **9.** I was a college girl in the Sixties.

_____ **10.** Is the new professor of asian or polynesian descent?

~ *18* ~

Abbreviation

TITLES

- Abbreviate and capitalize personal titles (*Jr., Sr., Esq.,* etc.). Abbreviate and capitalize professional designations (*R.N., CPA, CLU, PLS, CPS*) and academic degrees (*Ph.D., Ed.D., M.S.*) that follow a person's name. After a person's name, *Jr.* and *Sr.,* like *II, III, IV,* etc., are not set off with commas; all other designations are set off. Abbreviations of academic degrees take periods; abbreviations of professional designations such as *certified professional secretary, professional legal secretary, certified public accountant,* and *chartered life underwriter,* are treated as acronyms and are written without periods.

  Troy Sparks Jr. possessed many excellent attributes.

  Troy Sparks, Esq., possessed many excellent attributes.

  Winfred Parkinson, CPS, was one of the most efficient secretaries in this office building.

  Dr. Robert Williams coined the term *Ebonics.*

  Robert Williams, Ed.D., coined the term *Ebonics.*

ORGANIZATIONS

- The names of business, governmental, education, military, labor, philanthropic, professional, and other organizations or agencies may be abbreviated as acronyms:

AFL-CIO	FBI	IBM
TWA	AA	NAACP
CBS	UCLA	UN

- Designations of corporate status or structure, such as *Corp., Inc.,* or *PLC,* are not abbreviated unless they are a part of the official organizational name:

    Yancy, Inc., was founded in 1921.

DATES AND TIMES

- Abbreviate days of the week and months of the year only in lists, graphs, charts, tables, illustrations, or other such visual presentations where space is limited:

    Dr. Goldman scheduled me for foot surgery on Thursday, May 31.

- The abbreviations *a.m.* (*ante meridiem*) and *p.m.* (*post meridiem*) are used for expressing clock time. They use lowercase letters followed by periods. No space follows the first period.

    Will the training session be held at 9 a.m. or 3 p.m.?

- Designations of the United States time zones (Eastern, Central, Mountain, and Pacific) are usually abbreviated, using ST for standard time and DT for daylight-savings time when so desired:

ET	EST	EDT
MT	MST	MDT
CT	CST	CDT
PT	PST	PDT

EXERCISE 18.1

*Make all necessary corrections to abbreviations in titles, academic degrees, and time in the following sentences. If a sentence contains no errors, write **OK** in the blank.*

_____ **1.** Dr. Steven Mims's medical credentials are impressive.

_____ **2.** He named his firstborn son Marcus G. Woodson jr.

_____ **3.** Diana Jennings, CPA, passed the examination the first time.

_____ **4.** Is Jerrold, inc., an affiliate of Hankins corp.?

_____ **5.** We plan to attend the symphony at Bass Performance Hall on Wed., Oct. 12.

_____ **6.** The young men were initiated into the fraternity on Friday, June 15.

_____ **7.** The company brunch is scheduled for 10 am next Monday.

_____ **8.** A new movie premieres on Channel 8 at 7 p.m. Central Standard Time.

_____ **9.** Peterson, inc, was established in March. 2001.

_____ **10.** We plan to go to the Botanical Gardens at 9 am Saturday.

UNITS OF MEASUREMENT

- Common U.S. units of distance, length, temperature, weight, volume, and other quantities are usually spelled out. Abbreviations may be used on invoices, packing slips, and other business forms where space is limited. Metric units are abbreviated in most exact measurements. Periods are usually used after abbreviations of U.S. units of measure (such as *oz., lb., in., ft.,* and *mi.*); they are never used with metric abbreviations.

We hiked more than 12 miles yesterday.

The temperature gauge was stuck at 60 degrees Fahrenheit.

Info. needed to fill your order:

Wt.: _____ lb. _____ oz.

Ht.: _____ ft. _____ in.

The invoice clearly shows that you ordered the 2-pound 3-ounce size.

I bought a 500-ml bottle of spring water.

Cortez Peters Jr., world champion typist, typed over 250 wpm without making a mistake.

My car gets 44 mpg on the highway.

221

*Correct all abbreviation and measurement errors in the following sentences. If a sentence contains no errors, write **OK** in the blank.*

_____ 1. We keep our thermostat set at 75 degrees.

_____ 2. A bale of cotton weighs 800 lb.

_____ 3. The label read "Net wt. 26.5 oz. (750 Grams.)."

_____ 4. Did you know that 30 deg. Celsius is the same as 86 deg. Fahrenheit?

_____ 5. Murray brought a two-liter bottle of soda to the picnic.

_____ 6. I keep a 500-ml. bottle of spring water with me at all times.

_____ 7. The sofa is 6 ft. 8 in. long and weighs 79 lb.

_____ 8. The card was inscribed "Welcome Little Jo! Born 4/15/03, 19 inches long, 5 pds. 10 ouns."

_____ 9. We drove 47 miles to Fredericksburg, Virginia.

_____ 10. My new car gets 22 miles per gal. in the city and 30 miles per gal. on the highway.

ADDRESSES AND GEOGRAPHICAL EXPRESSIONS

·   In business correspondence, street designations such as *Street, Avenue, Place, Lane, Boulevard, Court,* and *Road* are spelled out. However, *Boulevard* may be abbreviated (*Blvd.*) if space is limited.

Mrs. Eleanor Jones
1373 Crawford Street
Fort Worth, TX 76119

Mrs. Lila P. McPherson
112734 Sam Westinghouse Blvd.
Denver, CO 80237

- Terms indicating direction (*South, North, West, East*) that precede a street name are spelled out. Compound directions such as *S.E.*, however, are abbreviated when they are used after the street.

> Mr. Roderick C. Linton
> 18383 East Neon Court
> Bristow, VA 20136

> Mrs. Billye Latson
> 6385 Burke Street N.E.
> Philadelphia, PA 18373

- The United States Postal Service recommends that the names of states be abbreviated using the official two-letter state abbreviations on all mail, accompanied by the ZIP code:

> Mrs. Annabella Ross Giddings
> 13433 South Burlington Road
> San Francisco, CA 94126

- A period is placed after each abbreviated word in a traditional geographical abbreviation. Only with the two-letter USPS state designations are the periods omitted.

> Fargo, N. Dak.   Fargo, N.D.   Fargo, ND 58121

- If an abbreviation that ends with a period comes at the end of a sentence that requires a period, use only a single period:

> My workshop presentation is scheduled for 9 a.m.
> I have long admired the work of Dr. Martin Luther King Jr.

Make all necessary corrections to abbreviations in the following addresses. If an address has no errors,
*write **OK** in the blank.*

_____ **1.** Ms. Jessica Hart

    1237 Constance Ln.

    Chicago, Il 60606

_____ **2.** Dr. Calvin Peters

    21874 Remington Tyler Blvd.

    Los Angeles, CA 90014

_____ **3.** Mrs. Linh Voung

    8214 E. Nash Court

    Fort Worth, TX 76119

_____ **4.** Dean Ndanzia

    7878 Idle St., Southeast

    Dallas, TX 75205

_____ **5.** Carson Lundgren, director of sales

    Cassidy company, Inc.

    5000 State Line Pkwy.

    Cincinnati, OH 45238

~ 19 ~

Troublesome Words

See Chapter 5 for discussion of the words *can/could, lay/lie, raise/rise,* and *set/sit.*

a/an/and

A is used before a word beginning with a consonant or a consonant sound:

> *a* window
>
> *a* union (*u* in *union* sounds like the consonant *y*)

An is used before words beginning with a vowel sound:

> *an* egg
>
> *an* hour

And is used to join words, phrases, or clauses:

> Reading *and* writing are fun.
>
> Marcus *and* Pete were close friends.
>
> She is very nice, *and* everyone loves her.

accept/except

Accept means "receive":

> I *accept* your apology.

Except means "other than" or "excluding":

> Everyone will go *except* Paula.

advise/advice

Advise (verb) means "give advice":

> Veronica will *advise* me again next semester.

advise/advice (*Continued*)

Advice (noun) is an opinion or a recommendation:

> Veronica gave me some sound *advice* this semester.

affect/effect

Affect is a verb that means "influence" or "change":

> Being in love can sometimes *affect* a person's judgment.

Effect (noun) is the result of a cause or an influence:

> Studying for the exam had a positive *effect* on her grades.

Effect (verb) means "bring about":

> The organization will attempt to *effect* changes in our bylaws.

already

> Already means "previously" or "before"
> We were already planning to go camping.

all ready

> All ready means "completely prepared"
> They are all ready to go take the examination.

among

> Among implies "three or more"
> Divide the chocolate cake among the three of them.

among/between

Use *among* when more than two persons or things are involved:

> Divide the money *among* the five of them.

Use *between* when two persons or things are involved:

> Divide the money *between* the two of them.

are/our

Are is a form of the verb *be:*

> *Are* you planning to go to London this year?

Our is a pronoun showing ownership:

> That is *our* cottage on the lake.

been/being

Been is the past participle of *be*. It is usually used after the helping verbs *have, has,* or *had.*

> We *have been* standing in line for hours.
>
> He *has been* standing in line for hours.
>
> They *have been* standing for hours.

Being is the *-ing* form of *be*. It is usually used after the helping verbs *was, were, is,* or *am*.

> We *are being* exploited!

between

> Between implies "two"
> This is between you and me.

beside

> Beside means "along the side of"
> Stand beside me when we reach the top landing.

besides

> Besides means "in addition to"
> What do you plan to do besides wash the dishes?

buy/by

Buy means "purchase":

> I will *buy* a new wardrobe this year.

By means "by means of," "past," or "before":

> We will accomplish this *by* the old method.
>
> Henry walked *by* her desk.
>
> She promised the report *by* noon.

can

Can refers to "the ability to do something"

I can stop doing volunteer work whenever I choose to do so.

farther/further

Farther refers to a greater distance:

You live *farther* from the school than I do.

Further means "to a more advanced point" or "in addition":

We will discuss your report card *further* when I return.

fewer

Fewer is used with "things that can be counted"

You paid fewer bills than your spouse.

good

Good describes a noun (adjective)

She is a good person.

hole

Hole means a "cavity" or "opening" (noun)

There is a hole in the ground near the pansies.

have/of

We sometimes pronounce *should have, would have,* and *could have* so that they sound like *should of, would of,* or *could of.* In writing, be sure to write *have* and not *of:*

I *should have* gone to track practice.

it's/its

It's is a contraction for *it is* or *it has:*

It's finally over.

It's been great seeing you.

Its is a possessive word that shows ownership:

The kitten licked *its* little paws.

know/no/knew/new

Know means "understand" or "be aware":

I *know* that you are a fake.

No is a negative:

You are *no* longer a friend of mine.

Knew is the past tense of the verb *know:*

I *knew* that he was a fake.

New means "recent," "fresh," or "unused":

She bought a *new* Cadillac CSX.

less

Less refers to "amount," "value" or "degree"

I have less money than you have.

lose/loose

Lose is a verb meaning "misplace" or "fail to win":

Don't *lose* your money betting on a horse that's sure to *lose* every race.

Loose is an adjective meaning "not fitting tightly":

My clothes are too *loose* since I lost weight.

may

May refers to "permission" or "possibility"

Yes, you may go to the movies Friday.

I may decide to take a vacation this spring.

passed/past

Passed is the past tense of the verb *pass:*

We *passed* three schools on our bike ride to the park.

Past refers to what has already occurred:

Helen is *past* president of the organization.

If the *past* is a valid guide, this method will work.

principal/principle

Principal means "first or highest in rank, importance, or value":

> The *principal* way to prevent spreading a cold is to wash your hands often.

> My uncle is the *principal* at the new high school.

A *principle* is an accepted rule of conduct action or a basic law, axiom, or doctrine:

> Democratic representation is based on the *principle* that each citizen should have an equal say in the political process.

quiet/quite/quit

Quiet refers to stillness or silence:

> Ashley was very *quiet* this morning.

Quite means "extremely" or "very":

> He was *quite* personable.

Quit means "stop":

> Last year I *quit* trying to be everything to everybody.

suppose/be supposed to

Suppose means "guess" or "assume":

> I *suppose* she can be trusted.

Be supposed to means "ought to" or "should":

> You *are supposed to* clean your room every day.

than/then

Than is used in comparisons:

> This package is bigger *than* the other one.

Then means "at the time" or "afterward":

> She was pretty *then*.

> We traveled to London, and *then* we returned to Dallas.

their/there/they're

Their implies ownership or possession:

> The Wilsons sold *their* house but took *their* furnishings with them.

There indicates a direction:

Look over *there*.

There also introduces a thought:

There is something strange about her.

They're is a contraction for *they are:*

They're planning to attend the banquet tonight.

though/through

Though implies a contrast:

Though we don't like her, we must respect her.

As though means "as if":

You looked at me *as though* you had never seen me before.

Through means "in one side and out the other," "finished," or "by means of":

The little girl ran *through* the park.

I am *through* putting up with you.

You can build endurance and muscle tone *through* regular exercise.

to/too/two

To implies movement toward another place:

We are going *to* the museum tomorrow.

To is also the marker of an infinitive:

To know her is *to* love her.

Too means "also" or "very":

I want to go *too.*

It's *too* hot in here!

Two is the number 2:

Two of us will accompany you to the museum.

use/used to

As a noun, *use* is a practical application. As a verb, *use* means "make use of." The past tense of *use* is *used*.

Of what *use* is this to me?

Let me *use* your orange lipstick.

Patricia *used* all of the butter.

As a verb, *used to* means "do habitually in the past." As an adjective, *used to* means "accustomed to."

She *used to* do everything that her friend did.

I got *used to* being alone.

weather/whether

Weather refers to atmospheric conditions:

Florida's *weather* is warm all year round.

Whether implies an unresolved question:

I will go *whether* you go or not.

well

Well describes a verb (adverb)

Does Robert feel well today?

were/we're/where

Were is the past tense of *are:*

Were you considering taking sewing lessons?

We're is the contraction for *we are:*

We're no longer taking him for granted.

Where refers to a location or place:

Where is my ticket to Bass Hall?

Where did you go last night?

whole

Whole means "complete" (adjective)

Give them a whole piece of apple pie.

who's/whose

Who's is the contraction for *who is:*

Who's the author of this wonderful book?

Whose implies ownership or possession:

Whose sunglasses are these?

your/you're

Your implies ownership or possession:

This is *your* life, so live it to the fullest!

You're is the contraction for *you are:*

You're kidding, aren't you?

ঙ EXERCISE 19.1 ঙ

Correct all errors with troublesome words in the following sentences. If a sentence has no errors, write **OK** *in the blank.*

_____ **1.** Ron is going to by a knew car this summer.

_____ **2.** Let me know weather you plan to attend the fiesta their having.

_____ **3.** Were is the article that you wrote for the newspaper?

_____ **4.** David walked passed my house and pretended that he did not see me.

_____ **5.** Please except my invitation to the masquerade party.

_____ **6.** You were suppose to be here by noon.

_____ **7.** I use to drink milk every night before retiring.

_____ **8.** Ashley likes spaghetti better than macaroni and cheese.

_____ **9.** Let's have a picnic in a quite spot beside the lake.

_____ **10.** An good friend of mine advised me to take World Literature II.

❧ EXERCISE 19.2 ❧

Underline the appropriate word in each of the following sentences.

1. Derrick finished the exam sooner (then, than) I thought he would.
2. (Suppose, Supposed) we sit down and talk things over before making a decision.
3. Is Constance planning to participate (to, too, two)?
4. The children ran (though, through) the park yelling and screaming.
5. (Your, You're) not responsible for the mistakes that he has made in life.
6. (Whose, Who's) essay was entered in the final competition?
7. The screw on the cabinet door was (loose, lose).
8. (It's, Its) about time you paid for lunch.
9. It has (being, been) a long time since we had steak for dinner.
10. (Were, We're) addressing envelopes at the meeting tonight.

❧ EXERCISE 19.3 ❧

Underline the appropriate word in each of the following sentences.

1. You (could of, could have) told me that before I made the worst mistake of my life.
2. They have (been, being) procrastinating for six months now.
3. Please (except, accept) my apology, and I will never do that again.
4. Sonia (passed, past) her history test in a few minutes.
5. I am not (quiet, quite) satisfied with your performance in this area of the competition.
6. (Your, You're) right on time for dinner.
7. My husband keeps a lot of (lose, loose) change in the console of his car.
8. He finally realized that (their, they're, there) not telling him the truth.
9. Mrs. LaRue's complexion is much smoother (then, than) Mrs. Meeks' complexion.
10. (Whether, Weather) you are guilty or not, there is a possibility that you will be convicted.

ॐ EXERCISE 19.4 ॐ

Underline the appropriate word in each of the following sentences.

1. (Your, You're) not doing as well this semester as you did last semester.
2. (Though, Through) the largest particles were removed from the sink, a lot of trash still remains in the pipes.
3. Haltom's is having a (loose, lose) diamond sale Saturday.
4. (A, An) hour has passed, and Cleo has not moved an inch.
5. (Whose, Who's) to blame for the misunderstanding?
6. All of your theory makes sense (accept, except) the last part.
7. (Were, We're, Where) in the process of renovating our house on the lake.
8. You (use, used) to worship the ground she walked on.
9. This information is (two, too, to) much for me to handle.
10. This will be (are, our) decision to make, not yours.

ॐ EXERCISE 19.5 ॐ

Underline the appropriate word in each of the following sentences.

1. Distribute the cookies evenly (between, among) the three children.
2. I (advise, advice) you not to take more than two classes while you are working.
3. Tyrone's (principle, principal) reason for missing school was not sufficient.
4. You are going to (loose, lose) your mind if you don't find some activity to occupy your spare time.
5. Gaining control of her finances has a positive (affect, effect) on her personality.
6. (By, Buy) me a new computer, and I will type all of your correspondence for two years.
7. Do you (no, know) that a portrait of Jim Bowie is being added to the historical collection in Austin, Texas?
8. The fox hid (it's, its) babies in the storage room.
9. Be (quiet, quite) or you will be denied assistance.
10. (Suppose, Supposed) you take care of your business and stay out of mine.

Underline each troublesome word that is used inappropriately in the following passage. Write your correction above the word.

Life Is No Bowl of Cherries

Who said that "life is a bowl of cherries"? Life has it's ups and it's downs. Either we can except it, or we can live in a dream world for the rest of hour lives. Now, last Friday was one of my down days. At the start, it promised to be a good one for me. But things didn't quiet turn out that way. First, I could of enjoyed a big, fat waffle for breakfast, but I didn't. I could of curled up by the fireplace while having my coffee, but I didn't. My alarm clock didn't sound, so I awakened 30 minutes later then usual. I scurried too my feet an dashed two the bathroom to get cleaned up and dressed. They're was know time to put on makeup; therefore, I just put on my clothes and dashed out the back door. I jumped into my car, turned on the ignition, backed out of the garage, an headed north. When I arrived at the parking lot were I normally park, I didn't see any cars. But I parked anyway. After all, it was a workday. Walking through the front door of the office building, I noticed that their weren't any familiar people in sight. The security guard addressed me, asking, "What are you doing here today?" I said, "Well, I'm suppose to be here. It's a workday, isn't it?" "No," he said, "today is Presidents' Day, and you have the day off." My jaw dropped, an I was more embarrassed then I had ever been in my life. I said, "Yes, that's right. I forgot." Turning slowly, I thought, I could of eaten those waffles and could of curled up by the fireplace. I walked across the street and got into my car. As I drove speedily on Parker Freeway, a car in front of me stopped suddenly, and bang! I rear-ended it. A tall, lean man got out of the car, checked it, shouted a few choice words, and returned too his car. Though their was know damage to his car, their was damage to my feelings. My face turned beet red, and I drove off when the light turned green. Finally, I drove into my garage, parked my car, and went inside the house thinking, "If life's a bowl of cherries, today I got the pits!"

❧ 20 ❧

Spelling

GENERAL GUIDELINES

- Underline words you are not sure of when you write your paper. When you are ready to write your final draft, look the words up in the dictionary.

- Use a computer spell-checker. But remember, a spell-checker cannot think. If you mistype one word for another, such as *and* for *an,* the spell-checker cannot make the correction. *Always* proofread your paper after using the spell-checker.

- Use mnemonic ("reminder") tricks that will help you remember the spelling of words (e.g., "The *principal* is your *pal*" or "*I* before *e* except after *c*").

- Keep a list of the words you misspell, and review it often. Practice writing the words several times.

- Test yourself. Use flash cards or have someone dictate the words from your list.

- Review all basic spelling rules from this book and other books that are at your disposal.

- Study the troublesome words in Chapter 19.

DETERMINING VOWELS AND CONSONANTS

Some spelling rules require that you know the difference between a vowel and a consonant. The vowels are *a, e, i, o, u.* All the other letters are consonants. The letter *y* can be either a vowel or a consonant, depending on the sound.

*Identify the vowels and consonants in the following words. Write **V** for vowel and **C** for consonant in the blank.*

Example: _CVCVCV_ secure

_____ **1.** justify

_____ **2.** downward

_____ **3.** piano

_____ **4.** queer

_____ **5.** bicycle

_____ **6.** healthy

_____ **7.** goddess

_____ **8.** victory

_____ **9.** zero

_____ **10.** xylophone

_____ **11.** keep

_____ **12.** waste

_____ **13.** yearn

_____ **14.** mumps

_____ **15.** fact

_____ **16.** X-ray

_____ **17.** steady

_____ **18.** presume

_____ **19.** juvenile

_____ **20.** easel

MAJOR SPELLING RULES

- *I before E*

  Remember this poem:

  I before e except after c

  Or when sounded like a as in neighbor or weigh.

  Niece is spelled *ie* because there is no *c* before *ie*.

  Receipt is spelled *ei* because there is a *c* before *ei*.

  Words with a *shen* sound are spelled with *ie* after the *c:*

  sufficient, efficient, conscience

- Exceptions to this rule are:

height	either	weird	foreign
their	neither	society	seize

❧ EXERCISE 20.2 ❧

Supply ie *or* ei *for each of the following words. Pronounce the words out loud.*

1. conven_ _ nce   **6.** perc _ _ ve

2. h _ _ ght   **7.** bel _ _ ve

3. cash _ _ r   **8.** d _ _ ty

4. effic _ _ nt   **9.** consc _ _ nce

5. l _ _ n   **10.** n _ _ ther

- When adding an ending to a word ending in a consonant and *y*, change the *y* to *i*:

    pretty, prettier
    lucky, luckier

- If the word ends in a vowel and *y*, do not change the *y*.

    pay, payment

Exceptions to this rule are:

    say, said
    lay, laid

However, when adding *-ing* to words ending in *y*, always keep the *y*:

    portray, portraying

Add the suffix shown to each of the following words.

1. betray + -ed _____

2. defray + -ed _____

3. funny + -er _____

4. play + -ing _____

5. happy + -ness _____

6. worry + -ing _____

7. bury + -ed _____

8. delay + -ed _____

9. gray + -ing _____

10. tarry + -ed _____

• When adding suffixes that begin with a vowel (*-able, -ing, -ence*), drop the final *e*. When adding suffixes that begin with a consonant (*-ly, -ment, -less*), do not drop the final *e*.

> come, coming (*Coming* drops the final *e* because the suffix *-ing* begins with a vowel.)
>
> price, priceless (*Priceless* keeps the final *e* because the suffix *-less* begins with a consonant.)

• If dropping the *e* before a vowel suffix would change the pronunciation of the word, the *e* must be retained:

> peace, peaceable
>
> singe, singeing

Add the suffix shown to each word.

    1. arrange + -ing _____

    2. define + -able _____

    3. excite + -ment _____

    4. face + -less _____

    5. tame + -ing _____

    6. share + -ing _____

    7. trace + -able _____

    8. base + -ment _____

    9. love + -able _____

10. mere + -ly _____

• When you add a suffix that begins with a vowel (*-ed, -ing, -er,* or *-est*) to a one-word syllable, double the final consonant if the last three letters of the word are consonant, vowel, consonant (c-v-c):

    drip, dripped, dripping

    thin, thinner, thinnest

Check to see if the last three letters of each word are consonant, vowel, consonant. If they are, double the final consonant and add the suffixes -ed and -ing.

	Last Three Letters	With *-ed* Added	With *-ing* Added
1. tap	_____	_____	_____
2. rot	_____	_____	_____
3. type	_____	_____	_____

	Last Three Letters	With *-ed* Added	With *-ing* Added
4. circle	_____	_____	_____
5. rip	_____	_____	_____
6. bat	_____	_____	_____
7. detect	_____	_____	_____
8. pretend	_____	_____	_____
9. jog	_____	_____	_____
10. post	_____	_____	_____

✥ EXERCISE 20.6 ✥

Check to see if the last three letters of each word are consonant, vowel, consonant. If they are, double the final consonant and add the suffixes -er and -est.

	Last Three Letters	With *-er* Added	With *-est* Added
1. slim	_____	_____	_____
2. deep	_____	_____	_____
3. broad	_____	_____	_____
4. short	_____	_____	_____
5. fat	_____	_____	_____
6. flat	_____	_____	_____
7. dim	_____	_____	_____
8. black	_____	_____	_____
9. mad	_____	_____	_____
10. hot	_____	_____	_____

When you add a suffix that begins with a vowel to a word of more than one syllable, double the final consonant if the last three letters of the word are consonant, vowel, consonant (c-v-c) *and the stress is on the last syllable:*

> begin, beginning
> expel, expelling

Note that the stress is on the last syllable in *begin* and *expel*. Therefore, double the final consonants.

↗ EXERCISE 20.7 ↙

Check to see if the last three letters of each word are consonant, vowel, consonant. If they are, double the final consonant and add the suffixes -ed and -ing to the words.

	Last Three Letters	With *-ed* Added	With *-ing* Added
1. commit	_____	_____	_____
2. conquer	_____	_____	_____
3. compel	_____	_____	_____
4. express	_____	_____	_____
5. answer	_____	_____	_____
6. offer	_____	_____	_____
7. confer	_____	_____	_____
8. deter	_____	_____	_____
9. pardon	_____	_____	_____
10. prefer	_____	_____	_____

- Nouns usually take *-s* or *-es* to form the plural (see Chapter 1).
- Verbs take *-s* or *-es* in the third person singular (see Chapter 3).

COMMONLY MISSPELLED WORDS

absence	category	examine	kindergarten
ache	ceiling	existence	leisure
achieve	cemetery	familiar	library
acknowledge	chief	fascinate	lightning
advice	choose	February	likely
aisle	citizen	financial	livelihood
all right	college	foreign	loneliness
already	column	forty	loose
amateur	comfortable	friend	magazine
answer	committed	furniture	maintain
anxious	completely	government	making
appearance	conceit	grammar	marriage
appetite	conscience	grieve	material
attempt	conscious	guidance	mathematics
attendance	conversation	hammer	medicine
autumn	cruelty	handkerchief	minute
awful	daughter	harass	mortgage
bachelor	deceit	height	muscle
balance	definite	hospital	naturally
bargain	deposit	hundred	necessary
basically	dictionary	husband	neither
beautiful	disastrous	imitation	nickel
believe	disease	incredible	niece
beneficial	distance	independent	ninety
bottom	doctor	instant	obedience
breathe	doubt	instead	obstacle
brilliant	efficient	intelligence	occasion
bureau	eighth	interest	occur
business	emphasize	interfere	occurrence
cafeteria	entrance	interrupt	omission
calendar	environment	irresistible	opinion
candidate	exaggerate	January	opportunity

optimist	recede	sincerely	vacuum
ounce	receive	sophomore	valuable
outrageous	recognize	straight	variety
pageant	recommend	succeed	vegetable
pamphlet	relieve	suppress	vengeance
people	religion	telephone	view
perform	representative	temperature	villain
persistent	resistance	tenant	vision
physically	restaurant	tendency	visitor
picnic	rhythm	tenth	voice
plausible	ridiculous	than	Washington
pleasant	right	theater	wear
policeman	safety	though	weather
possible	said	thousand	Wednesday
precede	salary	through	weight
prefer	scarcely	tomorrow	weird
preference	scholastic	tournament	welcome
prejudice	science	toward	whether
prescription	scissors	transferred	which
probably	secretary	trousers	woman
psychology	seize	truly	women
pursue	separate	twelfth	won't
quantity	sergeant	unanimous	writing
quarter	several	until	written
quiet	severely	unusual	wrong
quiz	shriek	usage	yesterday
raise	siege	used	yolk
really	similar	usually	your

Review Test
Chapters 16–20

A. Correct all errors with numbers, abbreviation, and capitalization.

1. 60% of the produce spoiled before reaching the market.

2. The servers at the elaborate wedding entered the ballroom carrying fifty gallons of punch.

3. Jack's flight is scheduled to leave the airport at nine forty-seven.

4. The 35th Reunion far surpassed all of the other reunions.

5. We returned our new Model nine hundred seventy-two freezer because it did not reach maximum performance.

6. We read many works from the 1800's in my literature class.

7. In the middle of the semester, we discovered that page four hundred thirty-two was missing.

8. The February twelfth payment was misapplied.

9. While vacationing in St. Maarten, I met 3 interesting young ladies, and they all spoke portuguese, french, dutch, spanish, and english.

10. Our contractors gave us the upgraded frigidaire elite range because he had over-stocked them.

11. Joan said, "scattered collections of old pottery filled the cozy cottage."

12. The original statue of liberty was first owned by paris, france.

13. Franer blvd. was originally named Sconer St. before the bus station was built.

14. When president george w. bush saunters into a room, it is evident that he is self-confident.

15. Many easterners believe that Texas never gets cold.

16. The History Fifty-Three Ninety-Four requirements are absolutely unattainable.

17. Manny has 175 quarters and 8 nickels.

18. I could see the fourth of july fireworks from the Marks Hotel balcony.

19. The infant weighed 6 pounds eleven ounces when he was released from the Herman Memorial Hospital.

20. George asked the substitute teacher how far earth was from the moon.

B. *Correct all errors with troublesome words and spelling. Four sentences contain two errors.*

1. Take my advise and sign up with a provider that provides a free wireless router and modem.

2. If you would of let me know the circumstances behind your absence, I would of let you use my class notes.

3. Is Michael Jackson slimer than Prince?

4. Judith's watch is completely different then Joan's watch.

5. We're were you when the clerk brought the outlandish grocery bill?

6. I didn't no all of the test answers, but I new enough to get by.

7. Who's shirt is it that your wearing?

8. Your marketing strategy is to extreme.

9. The singeing cowboy rattled a tune as he strolled down the supermarket aisles.

10. To except your apology would be pointless.

11. It is an inconveneince for me to ride with you and wait for two hours for you to get off work.

12. He divulged his principle source of income.

13. Confir with your accounting professor before you complete the practice set in case there are some updates.

14. Janice is luckyer than I am when we play cards together.

15. You have less problems than you had last year.

16. Nurse Pritchet said that she is feeling good today.

17. Keep the secret between the three of us.

18. He past me as he rushed to the dining hall.

19. Dominique was expeled for disruptive behavior in the classroom.

20. Your neice should be honored to have you as an ant.

❧ *Appendix* ❧

ESL Tips
English as a Second Language

Nouns

    Nouns are either countable or uncountable.

        Countable nouns refer to distinct items and have both singular and plural forms.

        Singular example: One apartment

        Plural example: Two apartments

        Uncountable nouns refer to a group or general category of items. Uncountable nouns are always singular and require singular verbs. Some uncountable nouns refer to a mass or to abstract qualities.

        Mass Nouns

education	water	milk
furniture	money	luggage

        Abstract Nouns

courage	integrity	bravery
advice	loneliness	honesty

Countable nouns should never be used with *a* or *an*. They are used alone with the word *the*, with *pronouns* or with *quality words* such as *a great deal of, some, any, less, much, little,* or *no*.

Alone	**Quality Word**
Clothes are expensive.	Some clothes are expensive.
I need advice.	I need no advice.

Countable nouns can be used in a countable sense by adding words or phrases that indicate quantity.

Your words of advice will be greatly considered.

The dog eats *two bags of dog food* in a week.

Determiners

All single countable nouns must begin with a determiner. Determiners are words that identify or quantify a noun.

Common Determiners

a, an, the	some, any, no, either, neither
all, both, each, every	several, enough
its, their	this, these, that, those
many, much, a few, a little	whose, which, what
my, our, your, his, her	

Some other common determiners are possessive nouns (*Joe's* hat) and numerals (one, two, three, four, etc.).

Use *this* and *that* with singular countable nouns or uncountable nouns: *that program, this helmet.*

Use *a few, both, several, many, these,* or *those* with plural countable nouns.

Examples:	a few apples	many pencils
	both packages	these sheets
	several cookies	those people

A, An, and **the** are determiners called articles. Use *a* before a noun that begins with a consonant. Use *an* before a noun that begins with a vowel sound. Deciding which to use—*a, an,* or *the*—depends on whether the information is known to your readers or listeners.

Use *a* or *an* with a singular countable noun whose specific identify is not known.

- I will purchase *a* car next week.

In this example, the readers or listeners will understand that you are referring to cars in general, not a specific car.

Use *the* if the identity is known or is about to be made known. *The* is used for all known nouns, whether they are countable, singular, or plural.

- I will purchase *the* car next week.

In this example, the readers and listeners will know what specific car you mean. You have previously mentioned this car in your paper or conversation.

- I will purchase the car that we looked at last week.

The readers and listeners will know what car you mean because the sentence identifies the specific car.

Verbs

Verbs are often followed by infinitives (*to* plus the base form) or the *-ing* verb form. Some verbs are followed only by the infinitive; some verbs are followed only by the *-ing* form; some verbs can be followed by either. Glance over the following lists for verbs you use often. You can practice saying them with the appropriate verb form.

Verbs Followed by an Infinitive

agree	manage
ask	need
beg	often
bother	plan
choose	pretend
claim	promise
decide	refuse
expect	want
fail	wish
hope	

I *expect to see* you today.

He *pretended to assist* with the chores.

Verbs Followed by an -ing Verb Form

admit	imagine
appreciate	keep

avoid	miss
can't help	postpone
consider	practice
delay	quit
deny	recall
discuss	resist
dislike	risk
enjoy	suggest
finish	tolerate

> I *dislike cooking* holiday meals.
>
> We *finished cleaning* late in the afternoon.

Verbs Followed by Either an Infinitive or an -ing Verb Form

You can use either the infinitive or the *-ing* verb form after some verbs; there is little or no difference in meaning.

begin	continue	start	hate

> They began to eat when the meat arrived.
>
> They began eating when the meat arrived.
>
> • Both sentences have the same meaning.

With a few verbs, the meaning does change:

remember	try	stop	forget

> Marcus stopped to buy groceries.
>
> • This means Marcus bought groceries.

Marcus stopped buying groceries.

> • This means Marcus no longer buys groceries.

Verb Forms Used as Adjectives

The *-ing* and *-ed* adjectives give different information about the nouns they describe. An *-ing* adjective indicates that the noun produces a certain effect on others. An *-ed* adjective indicates that the noun itself feels the effect.

The *boring* professor

> • The speaker produces boredom in others. The people listening to the speaker are the ones who are bored.

The *bored* professor

- The speaker feels the boredom. The speaker is the one who is bored. Here are some common *-ing* and *-ed* verb forms used as adjectives.

Noun Produces the Effect on Others	Noun Already Has the Effect
amazing	amazed
annoying	annoyed
convincing	convinced
disappointing	disappointed
embarrassing	embarrassed
satisfying	satisfied

Prepositions

Prepositions, which are listed in Chapter 8, combine with verbs and adjectives in specific ways.

Prepositions with Verbs

apologize *to* someone	fill *up* a gas tank
apply *for* (a position)	insist *on*
arrive *at* (a building or event)	interfere *with*
pay someone *for* something	object *to*
call *off* a scheduled appointment	reason *with*
call *on* someone *for* a visit	rely *on*
complain *about*	reply *to*
concentrate *on*	smile *at*
congratulate someone *on* something	specialize *in*
consist *of*	take advantage *of*
deal *with*	take care *of*
depend *on*	thank someone *for* something
explain something *to* someone	throw something *at* someone (who is not expecting it)
fill *in* individual blanks (blank spaces) on a form	throw something *to* someone (who is waiting to catch it)
fill *out* an entire form	worry *about*

Prepositions and Adjectives

Some adjectives are used with specific prepositions.

addicted *to*	grateful *to* (someone)
afraid *of*	happy *about*
anxious *about*	interested *in*
ashamed *of*	jealous *of*
aware *of*	proud *of*
confused *by*	responsible *for* something
content *with*	satisfied *with*
convenient *for*	shocked *at*
excited *about*	similar *to*
fond *of*	sorry *for*
full *of*	suspicious *of*
grateful *for* (something)	tired *of*

Order of Adjectives

When you use more than one adjective to describe a noun or a pronoun, use the following order:

1. judgment or opinion (wonderful, beautiful, intelligent, terrible, strange)
2. size (small, large, big, tiny, tall, short)
3. shape (square, round, circular, flat)
4. age (ancient, old, middle-aged, young, new)
5. color (red, yellow, blue, green)
6. nationality (Italian, French, Chinese)
7. material (paper, wooden, iron, steel, plastic)

Sentence Structure

In English, a subject must be included in every sentence. Other patterns that may differ from your native language involve using subordinating and coordinating conjunctions, forming questions, and making negative statements.

Using Although and Because

The subordinating conjunctions *although* and *because* should not be combined with co-ordinating conjunctions (such as *but* or *so*) or with transition words (such as *however* and *therefore*).

Incorrect:	Although they went to the movies, but they did not see the main feature.
Correct	Although they went to the movies, they did not see the main feature.
Incorrect:	Because you failed to meet the requirements, therefore you were not accepted.
Correct:	Because you failed to meet the requirements, you were not accepted.

Questions

To turn a statement into a question, move the helping verb in the statement and place it before the subject.

We *are* establishing a new club this year.

Are we establishing a new club this year?

If there is no helping verb, add a form of *do* and place it before the subject.

The professor filled the flask with sulfuric acid.

- Notice that *filled* indicates the past tense.

Did the professor fill the flask with sulfuric acid?

Negatives

Use one of the following words to form a negative statement:

never	nobody	no one	nowhere
no	none	not	

When you are writing a sentence with *not*, place *not* after the first helping verb in a sentence.

Ming Ho will go to the library on Friday.

He will *not* go to the library on Sunday.

If there is no helping verb, add a form of *do*.

They completed their assignment.

- Notice that *completed* indicates the past tense.

We *did* not complete our assignment.

- Notice that *did* indicates the past tense.

Post-Test

A. Circle the appropriate answer for each sentence.

1. (To who, To whom) shall I give credit?
2. Your intention (was, were) to falsify incriminating evidence.
3. Jogging, walking, and (to swim, swimming) are excellent weight-loss exercises.
4. (Were, Where) did the terrible accident happen?
5. Even though she had congestive heart failure, she looked really (good, well).
6. Chin Ho sawed (skillful, skillfully) through the hardest wood in the warehouse.
7. Under extreme circumstances, she (tend, tends) to overreact.
8. Wynn (was, were) unaware of anything around her.
9. (You and I, You and me) have the awesome task of delivering these pamphlets by noon.
10. Can we reduce our expenses by (1/4, one-fourth) percent this year?
11. The coach spread the word (between, among) the eight teammates.
12. Has (Fisherman's, Fishermans') Wharf reopened since the violent thunderstorm?
13. Tony admitted that his father (could of, could have) treated him better.
14. (Their, There) is absolutely no reason for your insolence.
15. Derrick (is, are) very friendly, but calculating.
16. Both suits (was, were) ripped to pieces.
17. Are you (quiet, quite) sure that this is what you want to do?
18. (60, Sixty) percent of those assembled agreed to the terms of the contract.
19. Ru Le and Grace were the (principal, principle) actresses in the senior play.
20. Life was quite different in the (1700s, 1700's).
21. If the music arrives by July (10, tenth), we can meet the deadline.
22. The worst case scenario would be to have (50, fifty) people at the party.
23. You are neither helpful (or, nor) considerate.
24. (Who, Whom) volunteered to work at the shelter this weekend?
25. The carnival coordinator insisted that the tickets be printed with (3-digit, three-digit) numbers.

26. All of the condominiums (is, are) vacant, except the one on the far end.

27. Why didn't you divide the crayons (between, among) the three of them.

28. Gloria has (fewer, less) marbles than Stanley has.

29. Le Long wasn't feeling (good, well).

30. I have (already, all ready) taken my medication for today.

B. *Insert commas and semicolons where needed. Mark the one sentence that is correct with a C.*

1. The owner of the pet store on Main Street ordered two lizards, four hamsters, and a cat.

2. They named the new law firm Goodman, Yancy & Marks.

3. My heart mourns your absence therefore you must return as quickly as possible.

4. The temperature was tremendously cold icicles hung from the rooftops.

5. That voice though unfamiliar has a calming effect.

C. *Insert colons, quotation marks, hyphens, dashes, and apostrophes where needed.*

1. Your opinion in view of the circumstances is not needed.

2. This Great Nation A Proven Account is a wonderful historical account of political parties.

3. Most lethargic people do not take advantage of the opportunities available to them, said Mrs. Pete.

4. The mens restroom is on the other side of the museum.

5. Twelve women, eleven men, and 9 children were trapped under the rubble.

6. Justin made all As on his mid-term report card.

7. Her name was spelled H o r t e n s e.

8. Have your prepared the two page report for Monday's departmental meeting?

9. The governors elect met in the Sundance Room.

10. I recognized Dan's 18wheeler when it passed the café.

D. *Insert parentheses, underscores, diagonals, periods, question marks, and exclamation points where needed.*

1. To prepare for the festivities, we need the following: 1 a piñata, 2 a snack stand, and 3 some games.

2. The time-sensitive package was delivered c o Jean Fulkerson.

3. I subscribe to Your Fitness and Health magazine.

4. Did Erin's wife tell him that he has a pretentious nature

5. Beware of unscrupulous people in this poverty-stricken neighborhood

6. Whew That was a close call.

❧ Answer Key ❧

Pre-Test

A.

1. whom 2. You're 3. swimming 4. Where 5. really 6. swiftly 7. cost 8. to 9. you and I 10. 1/8 11. among 12. Dr. Morrison Hughes 13. should have 14. They're 15. but 16. are 17. quite 18. Forty percent 19. principal 20. 1800s 21. 13 22. 19 23. nor 24. who 25. two-lane highway 26. except l 27. among 28. fewer 29. well 30. already

B.

1. Order the pens, pencils, paper, staples, etc., from the bookstore. 2. The name of the newly formed company is Yancy, Bates, & Matson. 3. The results of the tests were inconclusive; therefore, the physician insisted on more testing. 4. The CEO was fired amid allegations of fraud; the vice president kept his position. 5. C: The journal article, which received national acclaim, was discussed at length during the forum.

C.

1. My answer—on second thought—is no. 2. *The American Novel: An Historical Perspective* is available online. 3. "Providing a biased opinion is like providing no opinion at all," said Jeremiah. 4. Mary demanded that her siblings do the following: make beds, wash dishes, and vacuum floors. 5. The women's basketball team is sensational. 6. Malcomb is the ex-president of Foundations Abroad. 7. Some people spell Brittney, B-r-i-t-n-e-y. 8. The boy's jacket was returned to the lost-and-found department. 9. My sisters-in-law articulated well at the annual oral competition. 10. That 18-wheeler almost sideswiped us!

D.

1. In case of an emergency, please equip your car with the following items: (1) a flashlight, (2) snacks, (3) a cell phone, and (4) a blanket. 2. Mail the package c/o Jonathan Lewis. 3. Give accolades to the editor of <u>New Perspectives</u> magazine. 4. Should you reciprocate because she bought your lunch yesterday? 5. The FUBU Collection is still quite popular among teenagers. 6. Gosh! This road is dangerous.

E.

1. Whistling, skipping 2. Pointing one's finger 3. To feign illness 4. having recently moved into the neighborhood 5. Reminiscing the good times

F.

1. F 2. C 3. C 4. F 5. F

G.

1. CS 2. C 3. F 4. F 5. CS

Chapter 1: Nouns

Exercise 1.1
1. thing, concrete 2. idea, abstract 3. idea, abstract 4. idea, abstract 5. thing, concrete 6. idea, abstract 7. thing, concrete 8. idea, abstract 9. person, concrete 10. person, concrete

Exercise 1.2
Answers will vary.

Exercise 1.3
Answers will vary.

Exercise 1.4
1. C 2. P, General Electric Company 3. C 4. P, Will Rogers Coliseum 5. P, Dr. Henry 6. C 7. C 8. C 9. P, Denver, Colorado 10. P, Dallas Cowboys

Exercise 1.5
1. women, C; linen, C; silk, C; cotton, C; velvet, C 2. Julio, P; bathroom, C 3. Cowboys, C; horses, C; sunset, C 4. voice, C 5. farmers, C; fox, C; pest, C; danger, C 6. Mr. Lane, P; Wednesday, P; Friday, P 7. Dr. Yakimoto, P; spring, C; career, C; golf, C 8. nurse, C; Faranak, P; needle, C 9. Amon Carter Museum, P; May, P 10. Chemists, C; chemicals, C

Exercise 1.6
1. P, brothers-in-law 2. P, razors 3. P, runners-up 4. S, radio 5. P, governors-elect 6. S, session 7. P, men 8. P, trout 9. P, televisions 10. S, sister-in-law

Exercise 1.7
1. sunlight 2. essay 3. Le'Aisha 4. question 5. Ashley 6. Brunches 7. Determination 8. Destiny's Child 9. Teachers 10. Dinosaurs

Exercise 1.8
Simple subjects are indicated in boldfaced type.
1. <u>A cream-colored **cloth**</u> (in the buffet) will cover the Kwanzaa table. 2. <u>The handsome **man**</u> disappeared (into the night). 3. <u>Crystal **chandeliers**</u> lit up the entire ballroom (in the new building). 4. <u>The snow-capped **mountains**</u> (in the distance) were simply gorgeous. 5. <u>Rabid **rabbits**</u> were discovered (in the affluent neighborhood). 6. <u>The **cries**</u> (of the newborn baby) echoed (throughout the house). 7. <u>Violent **thunderstorms**</u> (near the Glenview area) frightened the residents. 8. <u>High-pitched **screams**</u> (in the distance) led us (to the culprit). 9. <u>**Calls**</u> (within the New York area) are discounted 5 percent. 10. <u>Rusty copper **piping**</u> (under the sink) caused the water contamination.

Exercise 1.9
1. *Mona Lisa*, paintings, world 2. fact, times 3. Salon Carré, Louvre museum, Paris, France 4. years, hotel, Florence, Italy 5. masterpiece, 1500s, Leonardo da Vinci 6. viewers 7. painting, experts, woman, viewer, meaning, smile, face 8. *Mona Lisa*, point, look, sadness, despair, face 9. point, viewer 10. matter, gaze 11. right, eyes, left 12. fact, painting, study, masterpiece 13. people, picture, portrait, Leonardo, woman 14. world, secret, *Mona Lisa*

Chapter 2: Pronouns

Exercise 2.1
1. It, my, it, yours 2. Your, mine 3. he 4. You, me, you, me 5. You 6. We, our 7. He, he 8. her 9. He, he 10. her

Exercise 2.2

1. his, he 2. their, you, them 3. his, he, he, his 4. Our, her, their 5. them 6. I, I, you 7. You, your 8. Her, his, they 9. his, he, it 10. mine

Exercise 2.3

1. he 2. He 3. His, his 4. He, they 5. his 6. his

Exercise 2.4

1. I 2. It 3. We 4. we, our 5. we, us

Exercise 2.5

Answers may vary.
1. mine 2. We 3. my 4. their, ours 5. My

Exercise 2.6

Answers may vary.
1. Who 2. Which 3. Whose 4. What 5. What 6. Who 7. whom 8. Who 9. Which 10. whom

Exercise 2.7

Answers may vary.
1. These 2. This 3. That 4. This 5. These 6. This 7. That 8. That 9. Those 10. These

Exercise 2.8

1. your 2. Whose 3. yours 4. Whose 5. Its 6. Your 7. Their 8. her 9. its 10. Their

Exercise 2.9

1. myself 2. himself *or* herself 3. yourself 4. themselves 5. herself 6. herself 7. themselves 8. ourselves 9. itself 10. yourself

Exercise 2.10

1. himself 2. ourselves 3. yourself 4. himself 5. herself 6. themselves 7. myself 8. itself 9. himself 10. herself

Exercise 2.11

1. Marcia 2. doctors 3. Investors 4. Joan 5. Demetrice 6. Henry 7. motorists 8. bird 9. actor 10. puppy

Exercise 2.12

Antecedents are in italics.
1. its, *one* 2. its, *one* 3. it, *either* 4. his *or* her, *neither* 5. his *or* her, *everyone* 6. his *or* her, *neither* 7. his *or* her, *each* 8. his *or* her, *one* 9. his *or* her, *neither* 10. his *or* her, *one*

Exercise 2.13

1. succeed 2. was 3. causes 4. knows 5. come 6. seems 7. screams 8. plan 9. abide 10. were

Exercise 2.14

1. He 2. She 3. He 4. I 5. I 6. I 7. He 8. We 9. They 10. He

Exercise 2.15

1. him and her 2. him and her 3. you and me 4. you and me 5. him and her 6. her 7. us 8. him 9. You and I 10. them, us

Exercise 2.16

Answers will vary.

Exercise 2.17

1. who 2. Who 3. whoever 4. Whoever 5. whom 6. Whomever 7. Who 8. Whoever 9. whomever 10. Whoever

Exercise 2.18
1. whom 2. Who 3. whomever 4. whom 5. whoever 6. whom 7. Who 8. Whoever 9. whom 10. Who

Chapter 3: Regular and Irregular Verbs

Exercise 3.1
1. C 2. S 3. S 4. R 5. S 6. S 7. Q 8. S 9. R 10. C

Exercise 3.2
Main verb is indicated in boldfaced type.
1. may have been **stolen** 2. Did **see** 3. Has been **introduced** 4. should be **arriving** 5. may **notice** 6. Do **know** 7. has **observed** 8. will **determine** 9. has **mastered** 10. Does **make**

Exercise 3.3
1. entered, past 2. practiced, past 3. scrambled, past 4. eat, present 5. sounded, past 6. assume, present 7. Call, present 8. scribbled, past 9. park, present 10. skipped, past

Exercise 3.4
1. are 2. is 3. is 4. is 5. are 6. was 7. were 8. is 9. was 10. Were

Exercise 3.5
1. has 2. have 3. have 4. were 5. is 6. are 7. have 8. has 9. Is 10. are

Exercise 3.6
1. wrote 2. worn 3. wrung 4. took 5. stolen 6. threw 7. sang 8. swore 9. taught 10. tell

Exercise 3.7
1. perfected, past 2. schedule, present 3. participate, present 4. blew, past 5. stood, past 6. attends, present 7. shone, past 8. completed, past 9. enjoys, present 10. changed, past

Exercise 3.8
1. charge 2. passes 3. walk 4. pays 5. answer 6. work 7. eat 8. eats 9. donates 10. tickle

Exercise 3.9
1. does 2. swim 3. wants 4. does 5. feel 6. becomes 7. does 8. look 9. does 10. have

Exercise 3.10
1. has 2. invited 3. began 4. went 5. landed 6. continued 7. choked 8. rolled 9. popped, fell 10. slurped 11. attempted 12. went 13. made 14. trickled, landed 15. lunged 16. licked, let out, got up, said 17. was glad, hoped

Exercise 3.11
1. Did tell 2. is 3. float 4. is bathed 5. refer 6. is 7. is 8. are transmitted 9. serves 10. is 11. can live 12. does 13. shows 14. remains 15. is, explains

Chapter 4: Subject-Verb Agreement

Exercise 4.1
1. S 2. S 3. S 4. P 5. S 6. P 7. S 8. P 9. S 10. P

Exercise 4.2

Subject is indicated in boldfaced type.
1. **officers** arrive 2. **You** look 3. **It** gives 4. **They** read 5. **Mary** watches 6. **she** makes 7. **He** turns 8. **evidence** is 9. **Donnie** stands 10. **She** ceases

Exercise 4.3
Subject is indicated in boldfaced type.
1. **Marguerite** enjoys 2. **Shaunette** plays 3. **marriage** appears 4. **justice of the peace** arrives 5. **documents** prove 6. **United Way** benefits 7. **printer** prints 8. **statement** appears 9. **marble** is 10. **Mercury** has

Exercise 4.4
Subject is indicated in boldfaced type.
1. **Italy and Greece** are 2. **John nor his friend** accepts 3. **Gloria and her brothers** were 4. **carpenters and contractors** meet 5. **Justine or Mark** has 6. **Hard work and determination** constitute 7. **Bernadette or Brian** was 8. **brooms or vacuum cleaner** was 9. **Sharon and her sisters** participate 10. **Jane or Frances** is

Exercise 4.5
Subject is indicated in boldfaced type.
1. **lightning** scares 2. **teachers** get 3. **Mitsuko or Stella** is 4. **Bacon and eggs** is 5. **children nor the parent** is 6. **musician or choir members** were 7. **electrician and plumber** work 8. **Tenacity and courage** are 9. **Cooking and cleaning** are 10. **Drinking liquor and smoking cigarettes** were

Exercise 4.6
1. Are 2. Were 3. Is 4. is 5. Has

Exercise 4.7
Indefinite pronouns are in boldface. Prepositional phrases are in italics.
1. **Each**, *of the teachers*, is, *in the festival*, is 2. **Everybody**, knows 3. **Both** object 4. **Everybody**, *in close proximity*, *to the school*, was 5. **Many**, offer, *to the two orphan boys* 6. **Each**, *of them*, causes 7. **Nobody**, tells 8. **Several**, are 9. **few**, are, *for the flea market, on Saturday* 10. **Someone**, steals

Exercise 4.8
Collective nouns are in boldface.
1. I, **faculty** have 2. U, **group** has 3. I, **board** vote 4. U, **committee** has 5. U, **unit** is 6. I, **class** have taken 7. I, **audience** were 8. I, **dozen** were 9. U, **cabinet** decides 10. U, **pack** eats

Exercise 4.9
Subject is indicated in boldfaced type.
1. **components** work 2. **She** persists 3. **everything** goes 4. **She** seems 5. Is **solution** 6. **convention** promises 7. **Peanut butter and jelly** is 8. **Disinfectants** were 9. **I** honor 10. **Television and radio** are

Chapter 5: Passive Voice and Consistent Verb Tense

Exercise 5.1
1. was fired 2. was given 3. was expected 4. was brought 5. was waited 6. was worn 7. were told 8. were given

Exercise 5.2
1. was watched 2. were given 3. was satisfied 4. was relieved 5. was delivered 6. were grown 7. was broken 8. were lighted 9. were considered 10. was parked

Exercise 5.3
Answers may vary.
1. awakened 2. ran, took 3. fixed, sat 4. was, took, left 5. got 6. picked, brought

Exercise 5.4

1. installed 2. signed 3. goes 4. walked 5. returned 6. told 7. did 8. captured 9. filled 10. surrendered

Exercise 5.5
1. lying 2. lay 3. Lie 4. laying 5. lays 6. lie 7. laid 8. lain 9. lay 10. lay

Exercise 5.6
1. lay 2. laying 3. laid 4. lay 5. lie 6. lying 7. lay 8. lain 9. lie 10. lay

Exercise 5.7
1. set 2. sit 3. sit 4. sit 5. sat 6. sat 7. sitting 8. setting 9. setting 10. sat

Exercise 5.8
1. Raise 2. rises 3. rise 4. have risen 5. rose 6. rose 7. raised 8. rising 9. raised 10. raise

Review Test–Chapters 1-5

A.
1. me 2. who 3. is 4. occurs 5. were 6. has 7. whom 8. retrieves 9. He and I 10. returned 11. are 12. its 13. laid 14. needs 15. Set 16. brothers-in-law 17. runners-up 18. fails 19. you would check 20. adhere

Chapter 6: Verbals: Gerunds, Participles, and Infinitives

Exercise 6.1
1. Reading by the fireplace 2. Waiting for a delayed airplane 3. Creating new procedural manuals 4. Avoiding your indebtedness by declaring bankruptcy 5. Prosecuting innocent people 6. Articulating the organization's purpose 7. Joining a Greek organization 8. Establishing credit 9. Dining in exclusive restaurants 10. Eating a balanced diet

Exercise 6.2
1. wrestling 2. harmonizing 3. driving long distances 4. drilling 5. watching the latest movies 6. deciding how to respond 7. bathing the small doll 8. drawing setting-sun pictures 9. singing soprano 10. seeing you cry

Exercise 6.3
1. b 2. h 3. e 4. d 5. a 6. i 7. j 8. f 9. g 10. c

Exercise 6.4
Referents are indicated in boldfaced type.
1. speaking in public, **talent** 2. parking in a handicapped zone, **misdemeanor** 3. juggling schedules, **task** 4. volunteering to help others, **quality** 5. working in the rose garden, **hobby**

Exercise 6.5
1. Grinning widely 2. Turning to the left 3. coming when it did 4. having seen the points of interest in New York 5. saddened by the student's comment 6. Impressed by the dynamic report 7. Disappointed by his girlfriend's indifference 8. shouting as he ran 9. interesting to most of the participants 10. Laughing loudly

Exercise 6.6
1. O 2. C 3. O 4. S 5. C 6. O 7. C 8. S 9. S 10. S

Exercise 6.7
1. c 2. d 3. g 4. f 5. a 6. i 7. h 8. e 9. b 10. j

Exercise 6.8

1. h 2. j 3. a 4. e 5. b 6. i 7. f 8. c 9. d 10. g

Exercise 6.9

1. P; Having been fishing 2. G; Painting a portrait 3. G; Playing a good game of golf 4. I; To lose 5. P; Jogging the 10-mile stretch 6. P; swimming the turbulent stream 7. I; To acknowledge excellent work ethics 8. P; Having completed your degree requirements 9. P; Circling the Pearson Multipurpose Center 10. I; To learn from one's mistakes

Exercise 6.10

1. C; Being an excellent pianist 2. P; Growing weary 3. P; Swimming in the limpid water 4. I; To determine the cause of the fire 5. G; Cooking delectable meals 6. C; Entering the contest 7. I; To avoid being caught 8. G; Planning the Alaskan cruise 9. P; Feeling ill 10. I; To travel to Europe this year

Exercise 6.11

1. To win at anything 2. to lose 3. (no infinitives) 4. (no infinitives) 5. To understand the feeling of the losers 6. (no infinitives)

Exercise 6.12

1. acquiring economic success 2. (no gerunds) 3. (no gerunds) 4. developing a plan of action; reaching this goal 5. Putting away a few dollars on a continual basis 6. cutting coupons from the Sunday newspaper; building a nest egg 7. using this method alone 8. limiting visits to restaurants 9. (no gerunds) 10. Paying $40 to $50 for a small lobster; planning to economize 11. tipping 12. saving through payroll deduction 13. receiving his or her paycheck 14. Saving a designated amount of money 15. planning economic success

Chapter 7: Adjectives and Adverbs

Exercise 7.1

Crossed-out words are in italics.
1. *more better,* better 2. *worse,* worst 3. *crazier,* craziest 4. (no change) 5. *bigger,* big; *wider,* wide 6. *mad,* madder 7. (no change) 8. *closest,* close; *higher,* highest 9. *more,* most 10. *sweeter,* sweetest

Exercise 7.2

1. D, That 2. P, Their 3. D, former 4. I, Which 5. P, Your 6. I, Whose 7. IR, Several 8. DR, whose 9. D, such 10. IR, which

Exercise 7.3

Answers will vary.

Exercise 7.4

1. g 2. j 3. a 4. i 5. b 6. c 7. f 8. d 9. h 10. e

Exercise 7.5

Answers will vary.

Exercise 7.6

Answers will vary.

Exercise 7.7

Answers will vary.

Exercise 7.8

Answers will vary.

Exercise 7.9

Answers will vary.

Exercise 7.10

Words modified are indicated in boldfaced type.

1. speedily, **drove** 2. peacefully, **lived** 3. 100 miles a minute, **runs** 4. there next to the piano, **lay** 5. gracefully, **glided** 6. awkwardly, **cut** 7. marvelously, **danced** 8. awkwardly, **ran** 9. graciously, **greeted** 10. because the coach is his father, **plays**

Exercise 7.11

Words modified are indicated in boldfaced type.

1. next to the Golden Gate Bridge, **stood** 2. deeply, **breathed** 3. because they did not pass the test, **were disturbed** 4. to lose weight, **dieted** 5. because she was more qualified than the other contestants, **was selected** 6. loudly, **moaned** 7. gracefully, **danced** 8. skillfully, **marched** 9. excitedly, **jumped** 10. awkwardly, **pranced**

Exercise 7.12

Words modified are indicated in boldfaced type.

1. very, **good** 2. painfully, **difficult** 3. totally, **spellbinding** 4. too, **conservative** 5. amazingly, **beautiful** 6. extraordinarily, **knowledgeable** 7. extremely, **talented** 8. very, **important** 9. exquisitely, **carved** 10. extremely, **thorough**

Exercise 7.13

Words modified are indicated in boldfaced type.

1. exceedingly, **well** 2. unnecessarily, **difficult** 3. very, **rapidly** 4. very, **well** 5. deeply, **embarrassing** 6. too, **slowly** 7. so, **painstakingly** 8. very, **quickly** 9. really, **soon** 10. tremendously, **well**

Exercise 7.14

1. Adj 2. Adj 3. Adv 4. Adj, Adv 5. Adv 6. Adv, Adj 7. Adj 8. Adv 9. Adj 10. Adj

Exercise 7.15

Answers will vary.

Exercise 7.16

1. quietly 2. quickly 3. really 4. well 5. poor

Exercise 7.17

1. huge, parking, neat, stately, brick, green, mature 2. nice, some 3. beautiful 4. dear, older, massive, concrete, fascinating 5. frail 6. her, every 7. her 8. gray-haired, elderly, surprised, little 9. nice 10. great, green 11. (no adjectives) 12. strangest, lined 13. (no adjectives) 14. (no adjectives) 15. wry 16. feisty, older 17. my, every, shifty, little 18. (no adjectives) 19. warm 20. busy, your, own 21. some, chocolate chip 22. old, my 23. good 24. nightstand, one, lone, half-eaten, bologna 25. (no adjectives) 26. new, navy blue, her, same 27. her, dresser 28. large, her, nice, nice 29. elaborate 30. beautiful, her 31. her, proud, her, happy 32. many 33. (no adjectives) 34. our, massive 35. bottom, new 36. her 37. That, my 38. my, sure, this, young, nice

Exercise 7.18

1. (no adverbs) 2. merrily, brightly 3. n't 4. (no adverbs) 5. hurriedly 6. (no adverbs) 7. frantically 8. (no adverbs) 9. (no adverbs) 10. (no adverbs) 11. loosely 12. inside 13. there 14. hurriedly 15. in there 16. hysterically 17. (no adverbs) 18. totally, far 19. (no adverbs) 20. just 21. very 22. n't, too, constantly 23. now 24. just

Chapter 8: Prepositions

Exercise 8.1

1. in a precarious situation 2. over the moon 3. around the corner 4. Due to extenuating circumstances 5. down the street, around the corner, into the courtyard 6. among them 7. across the grain, with it

8. During the winter months, of the time 9. in the flowerbed, nearest the house 10. at home, on account, of the weather

Exercise 8.2
1. c 2. d 3. f 4. h 5. a 6. e 7. b 8. g 9. j 10. i

Exercise 8.3
Answers will vary.

Exercise 8.4
Answers will vary.

Exercise 8.5
Objects are indicated in boldfaced type.
1. During, **morning** 2. after, **him** 3. with, **eyes**; by, **glances** 4. up, **mountain** 5. on, **Europe**; before, **book**; about, **lifestyles** 6. like, **idiot**; to, **center**; of, **room**; on, **floor** 7. on, **finger**; on, **wrist** 8. in, **chair**; about, **times** 9. from, **store**; in, **minutes** 10. until, **dark**

Exercise 8.6
The preposition in each phrase is in boldface.
1. **of** relief, **in** the room 2. **beyond** my faults 3. **off** the table, **during** the night 4. **down** the street 5. **throughout** the night 6. **of** the baby's head 7. **during** the intermission, **to** dinner, **after** the movie 8. **in** Florida 9. **within** his rights 10. **besides** read all day

Exercise 8.7
The preposition in each phrase is in boldface.
1. **of** bones and the cartilaginous and membranous structures, **with** them, **of** the body, **for** body movement, **in** this area 2. **of** muscles, fasciae, tendon sheaths, and bursae; **of** muscles; **along** the alimentary tract; **in** the heart 3. **of** the brain, the spinal cord, cranial nerves, peripheral nerves, and sensory and motor terminals; **of** the body; **with** the other systems; **with** the outside world 4. (no prepositional phrases) 5. **of** the air sinuses, larynx, pharynx, trachea, bronchi, and lungs; **in** bringing oxygen, **to** the blood; **in** eliminating carbon dioxide; **from** the blood 6. **with** the associated glands, **from** the lips, **to** the anus, **into** simpler substances, **by** the body 7. **of** urine, **of** homeostasis 8. **in** the pancreas, **during** pregnancy, **in** the chemical regulation, **of** body functions 9. **of** the ovaries, uterine tubes, uterus, vagina, and vulva, **in** the female and the testes, seminal vesicles, penis, prostate, and urethra, **in** the male; in the perpetuation, **of** the species

Chapter 9: Conjunctions

Exercise 9.1
1. and 2. and 3. nor 4. or 5. for 6. or 7. for 8. but 9. nor 10. yet

Exercise 9.2
1. but 2. yet 3. nor 4. but 5. for 6. for 7. or 8. yet 9. but 10. and

Exercise 9.3
Answers may vary.
1. and 2. but 3. so 4. so 5. so 6. OK 7. OK 8. for 9. but 10. OK

Exercise 9.4
Structures joined by the conjunction are italicized.
1. *Parallel parking was easy*, but *backing up was difficult* 2. *Good sense* and *sound advice* 3. *witty* and *wise* 4. *went around the corner* and *broke into the library* 5. *Charles* or *Otis* 6. *A hefty bonus* or *a raise* 7. *apply for the position* or *enroll in college full time* 8. *the airplanes are late* or *the flight attendants are rude* 9. *Learning to play dominoes* and *learning to play cards* 10. *The diamond was brilliant*, but *it was small*.

Exercise 9.5
1. but 2. and 3. but 4. yet 5. for 6. but 7. but, and 8. nor 9. yet 10. for

Exercise 9.6
1. nor 2. but 3. or 4. and 5. so 6. but 7. for 8. yet *or* but 9. yet *or* but *or* and 10. but

Exercise 9.7
Answers will vary.

Exercise 9.8
Answers will vary.

Exercise 9.9
Answers will vary.

Exercise 9.10
1. g 2. i 3. f 4. e 5. d 6. c 7. j 8. a 9. h 10. b

Exercise 9.11
Answers will vary.

Exercise 9.12
1. e 2. d 3. g 4. a 5. h 6. i 7. j 8. c 9. b 10. f

Exercise 9.13
Answers will vary.

Exercise 9.14
1. countries, they 2. player, you 3. patio, the 4. wobbly, Tarrence 5. dinner, I 6. exercising, I 7. spring-time, the 8. inferences, please 9. soon, you 10. repairman, we

Exercise 9.15
Subordinate clauses are in boldface.
1. Adv; **When I took my granddaughter to Sea World last summer**, she had a great time. 2. N; Tell me **whom you saw**. 3. Adj; Here is the book **for which I have been searching**. 4. Adj; This is the gown **that I want**. 5. Adv; **After the discovery of the lost gem was made known**, people stopped looking for it. 6. Adj; In the closet are the tennis shoes **that Veronica wore**. 7. Adv; I will get even with you **if it takes a lifetime**. 8. Adv; **If you take my advice**, you will not be sorry. 9. Adv; Your instructions were easy to follow **because they were clear and simple**. 10. Adv; **Though you left early**, you didn't miss a thing.

Exercise 9.16
Answers will vary.

Exercise 9.17
Answers will vary.

Exercise 9.18
1. however 2. hence 3. nonetheless 4. nevertheless 5. likewise 6. moreover 7. therefore 8. however 9. on the other hand 10. consequently

Exercise 9.19
Answers will vary.

Exercise 9.20
Answers will vary.

Exercise 9.21
1. yet, CC 2–5. (no conjunctions) 6. Though, SC; whether, SC 7. So, CC 8. (no conjunctions) 9. So, CC; and, CC; if, SC; that, SC; if, SC 10. that, SC; but, CC; that, SC 11. In the meantime, CA 12. that, SC 13. Although, SC 14. and, CC

Exercise 9.22
1. (no conjunctions) 2. Therefore, CA 3. also, CA; and, CC 4. Consequently, CA 5. (no conjunctions) 6. (no conjunctions) 7. However, CA; whether, SC; or, CC 8. (no conjunctions) 9. But, CC; and, CC 10. (no conjunctions)

Exercise 9.23
1. and, or, and, or 2. and, If, or 3. and, and, such as, and, and, and, that, and 4. Since, or, and, and, and 5. and, and, and, that

Chapter 10: Exclamation

Exercise 10.1
Answers will vary.

Exercise 10.2
Answers will vary.

Review Test–Chapters 6-10

A.
1. breathtaking 2. more dangerous 3. awkwardly 4. very 5. gray-haired, distinguished-looking 6. inside 7. fall, tomorrow 8. Small, tasty 9. first, striking 10. huge, roughly

B.
1. Ouch! 2. in, of, in 3. beside, near 4. and 5. over 6. about, on 7. on, above, of 8. Near, of, onto 9. and 10. of 11. hurt! 12. to, and, to, with 13. to, neither, nor 14. so 15. Beyond, of

C.
1. being human beings 2. Bowling, swimming, jogging 3. devastated by the student's remark 4. Screaming at the top of her voice 5. To argue over trivial things 6. Struggling to open the container 7. effectively 8. Dining in exclusive Parisian restaurants 9. Howling in the distance 10. To continue at this pace

Chapter 11: Fragments

Exercise 11.1
Answers will vary.

Exercise 11.2
Answers will vary.

Exercise 11.3
Answers will vary; the following are suggestions.
1. Heather enjoys attending college classes, especially her chemistry class. 2. She cooked the turkey and dressing, the green beans, and the potatoes. 3. I especially like reading science fiction. 4. For example, he did not understand the endowment. 5. All of the debts were paid except the ones that belonged to her husband. 6. We visited the ancient ruins and the modern buildings that were of interest. 7. The convention arena is filled with dignitaries, especially senators and mayors. 8. The professors completed most of the course syllabi, especially the developmental ones. 9. He also has a bachelor's degree from Prairie View A&M University. 10. Don't interrupt me when I am talking, especially if I am lecturing.

Exercise 11.4
Answers may vary.
1. We had a great time swimming in the crystal-clear water. 2. She did not see the policeman. 3. It was a very cloudy, dreary day. 4. Trying to get ahead in life, Roderick works from early in the morning until late at night. 5. She attempted to broaden her horizons. 6. I became very upset studying the details of the Civil War. 7. Reading the book with much enthusiasm, I forgot that dinner was cooking in the oven. 8. She did not realize the magnitude of the problem. 9. It is the key to obtaining the necessities as well as the luxuries of life. 10. Because she is very frail, she needs my undivided attention.

Exercise 11.5
1. To impress his peers, David bought the most expensive tennis shoes in the store. 2. He stepped up to the bench to deny all charges placed against him. 3. The king was very reluctant to relinquish his throne. 4. David repaired the leaky faucet to avoid having an extremely high water bill. 5. I completed the employment application to avoid upsetting my parents.

Exercise 11.6
Answers may vary.
1. Then she eats a large pizza. 2. Alice despises Alicia, but she pretends to be her friend. 3. It is easier if you plan ahead. 4. But she arrived at her swimming class on time. 5. Then we got lost.

Exercise 11.7
1. a; system, 2. a; criticized, 3. b; trial, 4. a; me, 5. b 6. b; court, 7. b; on, 8. b 9. a 10. a

Exercise 11.8
1. a 2. b; him, 3. b; seat, 4. b; evidence, 5. b; doctor, 6. a 7. b 8. a 9. a; *Menagerie*, 10. a; crime,

Exercise 11.9
Answers will vary.

Chapter 12: Run-Ons

Exercise 12.1
Answers may vary.
1. I own two mink coats, **but** I no longer wear them because I fear animal activists. 2. The majority of my time and energy is devoted to practicing, **but** it will pay off in the near future. 3. Procrastination is a dangerous thing, **and** it can cause many problems. 4. The likelihood of having twins is very slim, **for** twins do not run in our family. 5. I always meet my goals, **so** this makes me wonder whether or not I set them high enough. 6. People say that "absence makes the heart grow fonder," **but** this is not always a true statement. 7. Many people wish to become wealthy, **but** all I seek is to maintain a comfortable lifestyle. 8. The overwhelming evidence led to a conviction, **so** there was no way that he could avoid being sentenced. 9. Satellite television is a great invention, **but** I believe that it has thwarted communication within families. 10. I've read many great books, **but** *Testimony of Two Men* by Taylor Caldwell is my favorite.

Exercise 12.2
1. Escada and Ellen Tracy are considered high-quality clothing brands. **T**here are others that are just as good. 2. I have strong convictions concerning certain issues. **I** am nonchalant concerning others. 3. They are avid filmgoers. **T**hey never have time to visit with their neighbors. 4. Car accidents occur several times each day. **T**hey are not as dangerous as airplane trips. 5. Sticks and stones may break my bones. **W**ords will never hurt me. 6. Several articles of clothing were left in the bag. **W**e will donate them to Goodwill Industries if the owner does not claim them. 7. Chances are you will submit your paper late. **Y**ou will lose 10 points from your final grade if you do. 8. Van Cliburn will perform at Bass Performance Hall in June. **H**e is a great pianist. 9. Businesses are popping up all over town. **A** lot of others are closing their doors. 10. My husband has no problem with polishing silver. **H**e hates to wash dishes.

Exercise 12.3

1. California Cooper is a writer; she lives in Texas. 2. The lily is a beautiful flower; the rose is magnificent. 3. The novels are on the top shelf; the periodicals are on the bottom shelf. 4. Box seats cost more than the seats on the floor; I will settle for the floor. 5. Roberta stirred the cake with all of her might; her sister looked on in awe. 6. The stock market fell 10 percent in the first quarter; my father lost a lot of money. 7. Airplanes soar thousands of feet into the sky; they provide the fastest mode of transportation. 8. Peculiar things happen whenever she comes around; we try to avoid her. 9. Bread and butter go together; ice cream and pickles do not. 10. One friend is better than thousands of acquaintances; you are a true friend.

Exercise 12.4
Answers will vary.

Exercise 12.5
Answers will vary.

Exercise 12.6
Answers will vary.

Exercise 12.7
Corrected sentences may vary.
1. CS; Physics is a very difficult subject, **but** English is very easy. 2. FS; I'm cooking the dinner myself. I know that it will be a disaster. 3. CS; James Baldwin wrote *Go Tell It on the Mountain*. Charles Dickens wrote *David Copperfield*. 4. OK 5. CS; Mark is a computer analyst; Marie is an Internet engineer. 6. CS; Captain John Paul Jones said, "I have not yet begun to fight." Benjamin Mays said, "The man who outthinks you rules you." 7. FS; The fax machine belongs to me, **but** the scanner belongs to my sister. 8. FS; It takes a lot of determination to complete a college degree. It takes even more determination to complete a second one. 9. FS; He wrote an autobiography; **however,** we think that most of the details are untrue. 10. CS; The Waterford crystal was beautiful, **and** the Lenox china enhanced it.

Exercise 12.8
Corrected sentences may vary.
1. FS; Virginia taught Economics II for two years. **S**he taught Business Law I for five years. 2. OK 3. FS; The bride was 30 minutes late; the groom did not show up at all. 4. CS; Hannah loses weight easily, **but** her friend does not. 5. FS; Troy swims three times a day; **therefore,** he is an avid swimmer. 6. OK 7. FS; The savings bond matured, **but** we still did not have enough money. 8. OK 9. OK 10. FS; California is located on the West Coast, **but** I live on the East Coast.

Chapter 13: Dangling and Misplaced Modifiers

Exercise 13.1
Answers will vary.

Exercise 13.2
Answers will vary.

Exercise 13.3
Corrected sentences will vary.
1. DM 2. OK 3. DM 4. DM 5. DM 6. DM 7. DM 8. DM 9. DM 10. DM

Exercise 13.4
Answers will vary.

Exercise 13.5
Answers will vary.

Exercise 13.6
Answers will vary.

Exercise 13.7
Corrected sentences will vary.
1. MM 2. DM 3. MM 4. DM 5. DM 6. MM 7. DM 8. DM 9. MM 10. MM

Exercise 13.8
Corrected sentences will vary.
1. DM 2. MM 3. MM 4. DM 5. MM 6. MM 7. MM 8. DM 9. MM 10. DM

Chapter 14: Parallelism

Exercise 14.1
Answers will vary; the following are suggestions.
1. looking at the spectators   2. fishing   3. fine restaurants   4. up the hill   5. smiled   6. OK   7. OK
8. articulate 9. courteous 10. physically

Exercise 14.2
1. than 2. nor 3. and 4. but also 5. or 6. and 7. than 8. and 9. neither 10. or

Exercise 14.3
Answers may vary.
1. After the plane took off, the passengers talked, watched movies, read, and **slept.** 2. Both Fran **and** Candy were a little crazy. 3. He was neither happy **nor** sad. 4. The telephone repairmen are working in either my back yard **or** yours. 5. The Calvary went across the river and **up** the hills. 6. Neither the dean **nor** the professor would approve the student's reinstatement. 7. Either you will concede to his demands **or** move into another apartment. 8. You are not only selfish but **also** disrespectful. 9. I would rather attend the concert **than go** to the movies. 10. Jessica is not only talented but **also** resourceful.

Exercise 14.4
Set 1: Some choose to become (occurs five times) Set 2: who win . . . , who cure . . . , who concoct . . . , who specialize . . . , who design . . . Set 3: rich, famous, and recognized all over the world Set 4: cure our ailments, alleviate aches and pains, and save lives

Chapter 15: Punctuation

Exercise 15.1
1. Mrs. Smith, the guest artist, prepared an impressive display. 2. Please pass me the peas, potatoes, and bread. 3. The book is attractive, informative, and controversial. 4. She begged the domineering, meticulous assistant, but she was unable to dissuade her. 5. I went scuba diving last week, but I'm not eager to go again. 6. Jim Thorne, who lives on the North Side, asked for the opportunity to demonstrate his skill. 7. Our first annual family reunion is scheduled for Wednesday, July 12, 2004. 8. Realizing that she was not prepared for the recital, she feigned illness. 9. "Thanks a million, David, for bathing my poodle," she said. 10. Ling planned my trip, purchased my ticket, and drove me to the airport.

Exercise 15.2
1. The birdwatcher said, "That is a bluejay nesting in the live oak tree." 2. The two of them, Mr. Washington and Professor Yallow, arrived after the dedication. 3. The volunteers from the three schools (Bonner, Madison, and Parr) worked all day putting the project together. 4. On the other hand, we did qualify for a personal loan. 5. Werger, Brant & Eghart proposed a business plan that would benefit all of the companies. 6. The five young women simultaneously asked, "What does it cost?" 7. In the meantime, discontinue use of the prescribed medicine. 8. Paul, Marie, and Shamika are claims adjusters. 9. The three branches of government are the executive, legislative, and judicial branches. 10. "Let's get this party started!" shrieked the energetic, loud-voiced entertainer.

Exercise 15.3

1. A lot of talented, ambitious people entered the contest. 2. "The problem," intoned Mr. Joyce, "is that over half of the staff was late this morning." 3. It has been many, many years since the catering service opened in his father's name. 4. Mitchell A. Parks, M.D., became a volunteer fireman after he retired. 5. As agreed, Jane and Wong will write the article within one month. 6. The three decided, all things considered, to accept the changes without delay. 7. We added two new subjects to our curriculum last year; this year, three. 8. The father, not the mother, decided where the children would attend school. 9. The personal trainer purchased new treadmills, bicycles, and weights. 10. The seven continents are Europe, Asia, Africa, Antarctica, North America, South America, and Australia.

Exercise 15.4

1. Four best-selling books were purchased; however, no one read them. 2. Among those competing were Judy Scrup, Belleville High School; Clarence Taylor, Hogan High School; and Pete Latimer, Troup High School. 3. The bulletin board displayed the names of the winners; this was a great idea. 4. The payroll checks were not printed before lunch today; therefore, I was unable to pay my rent. 5. Ours will become one of the most advertised products in the nation: it will be seen via television, it will stand tall on billboards, it will be advertised in the newspapers, and it will ring out from radio stations. 6. Our itinerary requires the following stops: Turkey, Italy, and Greece. 7. He didn't leave the premises when the fire alarm sounded; on the contrary, he started talking on the telephone. 8. Success in the cosmetics industry requires the following: a nose for fragrances, a flair for makeup application, and experience in product research. 9. Dr. Martin Luther King was a civil rights activist; he demonstrated the nonviolent approach in resolving delicate issues. 10. Ronnie explained the process for painting a house: the painters need to make long, quick strokes across the wooden boards.

Exercise 15.5

1. "If Damon continues at this pace, we can expect him to become a star athlete," said his coach. 2. "We cannot," said Mr. Hord, "afford to pay these people." 3. The envelope was stamped "Confidential." 4. The court reporter read, "Yes, I am responsible for the error." 5. "Don't blame me for what happened," said Simone. "I'm only an innocent bystander." 6. I read the article "Living to Please Yourself." 7. Angelica's favorite song is "Evergreen." 8. Denise said, "That St. Pucci dress is gorgeous." 9. "The trailing purple petunias," he said, "look magnificent on the deck." 10. Danté exclaimed, "The brisk wind moved through the branches of the pine trees."

Exercise 15.6

1. What out-of-date clothes she wore to work today! 2. The 20-acre lot provides enough space to build a huge apartment building. 3. Will eighty-five table settings suffice for the convention dinner? 4. Please fix the railings on the fifth-, sixth-, and seventh-floor balconies. 5. Her sister-in-law has no luck when it comes to keeping a job.

Exercise 15.7

1. The teacher—realizing that the student needed remediation, counseling, and financial assistance—made every effort to help. 2. The newspaper, the radio, and the television—all are reliable news sources. 3. The four pilots—Rudy Scott, Malcolm Knox, Roger Chan, and Kent Ward—attended the same training school. 4. The elite of the group assembled to make plans for the reception—the others were not concerned. 5. The ballroom furniture—tables and chairs—have been refinished. 6. His only concern was his looks— in other words, what he would wear on his date. 7. Someday—mark my words—you'll be sorry that you didn't learn a trade. 8. "One's aim ought always be to leave that which one touches better than he found it"—at least according to Benjamin Mays. 9. My favorite meal—grilled salmon—is on the menu today. 10. Her only human frailty—or so she thinks—is criticizing others.

Exercise 15.8

1. Conner got all **A's** and **B's** on his report card. 2. I **won't** be needing these old **CDs** much longer. 3. The **Joneses'** dentist . . . 4. **Betty's** . . . 5. The **children's** sandbox . . .

Exercise 15.9

1. The term of the loan was thirty (30) days. 2. Follow these instructions carefully: (1) remove film, (2) cover with a paper towel, (3) place in the center of the microwave, and (4) microwave on high for 45 seconds. 3. The repairmen (if you want to call them that) couldn't repair my leaky faucet. 4. She's quitting her job tomorrow (what a joke) because she didn't receive a promotion. 5. A sentence must contain at least one main (independent) clause.

Exercise 15.10

1. Mark Delano stars in the television show **Moonlight**. 2. Mr. Wilkins always misuses the words **except** and **accept**. 3. The utility stock has decreased 1/2 percent this month. 4. Articles in the **Patent Attorney** newsletter are always interesting. 5. Please send me a copy of the book **Moby Dick** by Herman Melville. 6. You must purchase Dante's new album, **Drastic Measures**. 7. Tara's favorite rhyme starts out, "Three blind mice, / Three blind mice, / See how they run, / See how they run." 8. **The Scarlet Letter** is a book that I read many years ago. 9. I season green beans with onions and/or shallots. 10. In what year did **Midnight Cowboy** win the Oscar as best picture?

Exercise 15.11

1. I would ask what impelled them to separate, wouldn't you? 2. Whew! This office is stuffy. 3. They delivered the package c.o.d. yesterday. 4. What is the possibility of acquiring a federal loan? A grant? A fellowship? 5. Gosh! This is scary! 6. His father put the treadmill in the attic because he wasn't using it. 7. What a day! 8. Who was responsible for the problems we experienced? 9. I give up! 10. I get on North Blvd. where it intersects with Hillman Ave. near the county line, right?

Review Test–Chapters 11-15

A.

1. F 2. C 3. C 4. F 5. F 6. F 7. F 8. F 9. F 10. F 11. C 12. F 13. F 14. C 15. F

B.

1. F 2. C 3. C 4. CS 5. F 6. F 7. CS 8. C 9. C 10. F 11. C 12. CS 13. CS 14. C 15. C

C.

1. MM 2. DM 3. MM 4. C 5. MM

D.

1. by the giant white wall 2. walking 3. flutist 4. OK 5. OK 6. OK 7. passageway 8. OK 9. to decide 10. dancing

E.

1. The bank is unable to give you a loan; you don't have any tangible assets. 2. Our homeowners insurance offers protection from fire and natural disasters; it offers no mold coverage. 3. My co-worker is African-American; my pastor is Hispanic; and my cousin is Anglo Saxon. 4. Put the Oriental vase, the crystal glasses, and the antique china in the cabinet. 5. My first daughter, Marie, is nine; my second daughter, Peggy, is five; and my son, Dexter, is one. 6. All entrants must be witty, fun-loving individuals with pleasing personalities. 7. Rickety knees are a family characteristic; high cholesterol is also. 8. Graduation is set for May 15, 2005. 9. The movie, a great comedy, will air two weeks from today. 10. Alexander said, "The fraternity must comply with the university rules." 11. I can, if given the opportunity, succeed in my career of choice. 12. Henry enjoys exhilarating motorcycle rides, breathtaking helicopter rides, and life-threatening hiking excursions. 13. As agreed, customers must pay parking fees before 5 p.m. weekdays. 14. The architectural style of the buildings at San Marco in Italy, the Louvre Museum in France, and the ruins of the Acropolis in Greece are astounding. 15. Discrepancies are directly related to irresponsible employees within the department; layoffs are imminent.

F.

1. James's digestive system is out of whack. 2. You should—on second thought—consider the possibility of leasing a larger vehicle. 3. The Jones' 18-wheeler truck was repossessed because they failed to make timely payments. 4. The men's line of clothing is more popular than the women's line at this particular store. 5. My brother-in-law swindled his brothers and sisters out of a fortune. 6. She spelled her name a-s-h-l-e-e. 7. My ex-professor lectured nonstop with much zeal and enthusiasm. 8. The following items are needed for the picnic on Saturday: pickles, mustard, and buns. 9. The two-page articles reprinted in May, September, and December proved to be very popular. 10. The literary reference should be written Worthword: Altrusa Books, 2005. 11. *How to Lose Weight in Two Days: A Practical Workbook* arrived at the bookstore yesterday. 12. "There is," said Mr. Ramsey, "something strange about that young man sitting in the corner." 13. Dominque replied, "It was not my intention to cause dissension among the members of the committee." 14. The supervisor demanded a day-by-day account of the inventory. 15. "There is a possibility that I will delete some of the assignments," said the professor.

G.

1. When you travel outside the county, be sure to take the following items: (1) a passport, (2) an ATM card, and (3) some cash. 2. John's retirement check was sent c/o Mrs. Effie Smith. 3. The personal trainer distributed a copy of The Young and Fit magazine to all of the young women in the group. 4. Do you think it's just a figment of his imagination? 5. It was decided that 1/4 of the funds would be donated to the alumni association. 6. In all honesty, what is your opinion of the decision to hire a secretary with no computer experience? 7. One of the best novels of all time is The Scarlet Letter. 8. Wow! That news spread like wild fire. 9. Does she have a Ph.D. in English or math? 10. By the end of the day, the temperature was 100.6 degrees Fahrenheit.

Chapter 16: Numbers

Exercise 16.1
1. OK 2. four hundred 3. OK 4. one 5. Eighty-three 6. OK 7. OK 8. 12 9. 5s 10. $11,535,000

Exercise 16.2
1. 93 2. twenty 3. five 4. 2 pounds 3 ounces 5. 37

Exercise 16.3
1. 2 2. 5 3. two 4. 30 5. OK 6. 4 7. OK 8. OK 9. OK 10. 2

Exercise 16.4
1. four 2. OK 3. OK 4. 3 5. OK

Exercise 16.5
1. $1,000 2. $5 3. 55 4. OK 5. OK 6. 19 7. percent 8. three-quarters *or* three-fourths 9. ¼-inch 10. 2½ miles

Exercise 16.6
1. three, five 2. 30th 3. OK 4. noon. (omit *p.m.*) 5. two 6. OK 7. 12 8. 72 9. OK 10. OK

Exercise 16.7
1. thirty-two 2. 39 years 11 months and 22 days 3. eleventh 4. One 5. OK 6. Seventh 7. 33rd 8. OK 9. 22nd 10. twentieth

Exercise 16.8
1. OK 2. Eight, two 3. OK *or* a total of 523 4. 775 5. 23 6. 66 7. A total of 28,382,000 8. Second 9. three, two 10. 393, 194, one-syllable, 65, three-syllable

Exercise 16.9
1. August 14 2. April 14, two, May 8 3. 325, 25 4. OK 5. OK 6. 7, 35th 7. 8, 13 8. Fourteen 9. OK 10. 12,000

Exercise 16.10
1. Right 2. Right 3. Wrong; <u>$3.00</u> 4. Wrong; <u>$.35</u> 5. Right 6. Wrong; <u>thirty</u> 7. Right 8. Right
9. Wrong; <u>seven</u> 10. Right

Exercise 16.11
1. OK 2. OK 3. ⅛-inch 4. 12½ 5. 120 to 9

Chapter 17: Capitalization

Exercise 17.1
1. You 2. Ramona 3. Mountain Meadows 4. Maytag 5. Mark 6. OK 7. Trane 8. The 9. Cecilia
10. Amana

Exercise 17.2
1. Ph.D. 2. OK 3. OK 4. OK 5. Uncle 6. Princess 7. Professor 8. former 9. late 10. *Beauty, Beast*

Exercise 17.3
1. Carnivorous Animals 2. Literature 3. Ph.D. 4. OK 5. OK 6. Department 7. National Education
Association 8. American Literature 9. Living, Pennies 10. Ed.D.

Exercise 17.4
1. Central Park 2. Texas, Southwest 3. Windy City 4. West 5. OK 6. OK 7. French 8. Revolutionary
War 9. sixties 10. Asian, Polynesian

Chapter 18: Abbreviation

Exercise 18.1
1. OK 2. Jr. 3. OK 4. Inc., Corp. 5. Wednesday, October 6. OK 7. a.m. 8. CST 9. Inc.; March *or* Mar.
10. a.m.

Exercise 18.2
1. OK 2. pounds 3. (750 g) 4. degrees, degrees 5. 2-l 6. 500-ml 7. feet, inches, pounds 8. pounds,
ounces 9. OK 10. 22 mpg, 30 mpg

Exercise 18.3
1. Lane, IL 2. Boulevard 3. OK 4. Street, S.E. 5. Director of Sales, Parkway

Chapter 19: Troublesome Words

Exercise 19.1
1. buy, new 2. whether, they're 3. Where 4. past 5. accept 6. supposed 7. used 8. OK 9. quiet
10. A

Exercise 19.2
1. than 2. Suppose 3. too 4. through 5. You're 6. Whose 7. loose 8. It's 9. been 10. We're

Exercise 19.3
1. could have 2. been 3. accept 4. passed 5. quite 6. You're 7. loose 8. they're 9. than 10. Whether

Exercise 19.4
1. You're 2. Though 3. loose 4. An 5. Who's 6. except 7. We're 8. used 9. too 10. our

Exercise 19.5
1. among 2. advise 3. principal 4. lose 5. effect 6. Buy 7. know 8. its 9. quiet 10. Suppose

Exercise 19.6

1. (no errors) 2. its, its 3. accept, our 4. (no errors) 5. (no errors) 6. quite 7. could have 8. could have 9. than 10. to, and, to 11. There, no 12. and 13. where 14. (no errors) 15. (no errors) 16. there 17. (no errors) 18. supposed 19. (no errors) 20. and, than 21. (no errors) 22. could have, could have 23. (no errors) 24. (no errors) 25. to 26. there, no, there 27. (no errors) 28. (no errors)

Chapter 20: Spelling

Exercise 20.1

1. cvcccvc 2. cvcccvcc 3. cvvcv 4. cvvvc 5. cvcvccv 6. cvvcccv 7. cvccvcc 8. cvccvcv 9. cvcv 10. cvcvccvcv 11. cvvc 12. cvccv 13. cvvcc 14. cvccc 15. cvcc 16. c-cvv 17. ccvvcv 18. ccvcvcv 19. cvcvcvcv 20. vvcvc

Exercise 20.2

1. ie 2. ei 3. ie 4. ie 5. ie 6. ei 7. ie 8. ei 9. ie 10. ei

Exercise 20.3

1. betrayed 2. defrayed 3. funnier 4. playing 5. happiness 6. worrying 7. buried 8. delayed 9. graying 10. tarrying

Exercise 20.4

1. arranging 2. definable 3. excitement 4. faceless 5. taming 6. sharing 7. traceable 8. basement 9. lovable 10. merely

Exercise 20.5

1. tap tapped tapping 2. rot rotted rotting 3. ype typed typing 4. cle circled circling 5. rip ripped ripping 6. bat batted batting 7. ect detected detecting 8. end pretended pretending 9. jog jogged jogging 10. ost posted posting

Exercise 20.6

1. lim slimmer slimmest 2. eep deeper deepest 3. oad broader broadest 4. ort shorter shortest 5. fat fatter fattest 6. lat flatter flattest 7. dim dimmer dimmest 8. ack blacker blackest 9. mad madder maddest 10. hot hotter hottest

Exercise 20.7

1. mit committed committing 2. uer conquered conquering 3. pel compelled compelling 4. ess expressed expressing 5. wer answered answering 6. fer offered offering 7. fer conferred conferring 8. ter deterred deterring 9. don pardoned pardoning 10. fer preferred preferring

Review Test - Chapters 16-20

A.

1. **Sixty** percent of the produce spoiled before reaching the market. 2. The servers at the elaborate wedding entered the ballroom carrying **50** gallons of punch. 3. Jack's flight is scheduled to leave the airport at **9:47**. 4. The **Thirty-fifth** Reunion far surpassed all of the other reunions. 5. We returned our new Model **972** freezer because it did not reach maximum performance. 6. We read many works from the **1800s** in my literature class. 7. In the middle of the semester, we discovered that page **432** was missing. 8. The February **12** payment was misapplied. 9. While vacationing in St. Maarten, I met three interesting young ladies, and they all spoke **P**ortuguese, **F**rench, **D**utch, **S**panish, and **E**nglish. 10. Our contractors gave us the upgraded **F**rigidaire Elite range because he had overstocked them. 11. Joan said, "**S**cattered collections of old pottery filled the cozy cottage." 12. The original **S**tatue of Liberty was first owned by **P**aris, France. 13. Franer **B**lvd. was originally named Sconer St. before the bus station was built. 14. When President **G**eorge **W. B**ush saunters into a room, it is evident that he is self-confident. 15. Many **E**asterners believe that Texas never gets cold. 16. The History **5394** requirements are absolutely unattainable. 17. Manny has 175 quarters and **eight** nickels. 18. I could see the **F**ourth of **J**uly fireworks from the Marks Hotel balcony. 19. The

infant weighed **6 lb. 11 oz.** when he was released from the Herman Memorial Hospital. 20. George asked the substitute teacher how far Earth was from the moon.

B.
1. Take my **advice** and sign up with a provider that provides a free wireless router and modem. 2. If you would **have** let me know the circumstances behind your absence, I would have let you use my class notes. 3. Is Michael Jackson **slimmer** than Prince? 4. Judith's watch is completely different **than** Joan's watch. 5. **Where** were you when the clerk brought the outlandish grocery bill? 6. I didn't **know** all of the test answers, but I **knew** enough to get by. 7. **Whose** shirt is it that **you're** wearing? 8. Your marketing strategy is **too** extreme. 9. The **singing** cowboy rattled a tune as he strolled down the supermarket aisles. 10. To **accept** your apology would be pointless. 11. It is an **inconvenience** for me to ride with you and wait for two hours for you to get off work. 12. He divulged his **principal** source of income. 13. **Confer** with your accounting professor before you complete the practice set in case there are some updates. 14. Janice is **luckier** than I am when we play cards together. 15. You have **fewer** problems than you had last year. 16. Nurse Pritchet said that she is feeling **well** today. 17. Keep the secret **among** the three of us. 18. He **passed** me as he rushed to the dining hall. 19. Dominique was **expelled** for disruptive behavior in the classroom. 20. Your **niece** should be honored to have you as an **aunt**.

Post-Test

A.
1. To whom 2. was 3. swimming 4. Where 5. well 6. skillfully 7. tends 8. was 9. You and I 10. 1/4 11. among 12. Fisherman's 13. could have 14. There 15. is 16. were 17. quite 18. Sixty 19. principal 20. 1700s 21. 10 22. 50 23. nor 24. Who 25. three-digit 26. are 27. among 28. fewer 29. well 30. already

B.
1. C: The owner of the pet store on Main Street ordered two lizards, four hamsters, and a cat. 2. They named the new law firm Goodman, Yancy, & Marks. 3. My heart mourns your absence; therefore, you must return as quickly as possible. 4. The temperature was tremendously cold; icicles hung from the rooftops. 5. That voice, though unfamiliar, has a calming effect.

C.
1. Your opinion—in view of the circumstances—is not needed. 2. This Great Nation: A Proven Account is a wonderful historical account of political parties. 3. "Most lethargic people do not take advantage of the opportunities available to them," said Mrs. Pete. 4. The men's restroom is on the other side of the museum. 5. C: Twelve women, eleven men, and nine children were trapped under the rubble. 6. Justin made all A's on his mid-term report card. 7. Her name was spelled H-o-r-t-e-n-s-e. 8. Have your prepared the two-page report for Monday's departmental meeting? 9. The governors-elect met in the Sundance Room. 10. I recognized Dan's 18-wheeler when it passed the café.

D.
1. To prepare for the festivities, we need the following: (1) a piñata, (2) a snack stand, and (3) some games. 2. The time-sensitive package was delivered c/o Jean Fulkerson. 3. I subscribe to Your Fitness and Health magazine. 4. Did Erin's wife tell him that he has a pretentious nature? 5. Beware of unscrupulous people in this poverty-stricken neighborhood. 6. Whew! That was a close call.